The Little Book of Big Gains

THE LITTLE BOOK OF BIG GAINS

A GUIDE TO INVESTING WISELY

Sandeep Tyagi

BLOOMSBURY
NEW DELHI • LONDON • OXFORD • NEW YORK • SYDNEY

BLOOMSBURY INDIA
Bloomsbury Publishing India Pvt. Ltd
Second Floor, LSC Building No. 4, DDA Complex, Pocket C – 6 & 7,
Vasant Kunj, New Delhi, 110070

BLOOMSBURY, BLOOMSBURY INDIA and the Diana logo
are trademarks of Bloomsbury Publishing Plc

First published in India 2024
This edition published 2024

ISBN: PB: 978-93-56406-97-1; eBook: 978-93-56409-56-9
2 4 6 8 10 9 7 5 3 1

Typeset in Adobe Caslon Pro by Manipal Technologies Limited
Printed and bound in India by Gopsons Papers Pvt. Ltd., Noida

FSC www.fsc.org MIX Paper | Supporting responsible forestry FSC® C191020

To

Dr S.C. Tyagi, my father,

and

Mrs Subhadra Tyagi, my mother,

who gave me the confidence to learn new things

and

who were the first investors to trust me

Contents

Preface

On 20 October 2006, I became rich. Inductis, the company I founded in 2000 had been merged with another firm, EXL Service, and EXL Service went public on NASDAQ. My stake was worth a good amount of money. Major Wall Street firms were advising me on how to invest and manage my wealth. Then came 2008 and, despite some of the best advice, I lost almost 50% of my wealth. That was painful. And very stressful.

I realized that if I didn't build my knowledge to understand how to invest properly, I would always have a leaky bucket. I could keep earning more and keep putting it in the bucket, but if the leak was not fixed, everything would simply drain away. That was not a comfortable feeling. So as my next venture I set up an investment management firm, Estee Advisors.

Over the past 15 years, Estee Advisors has built several investment products with some remarkable returns on investment. It has developed algorithms to digest second-by-second data from thousands of securities transactions and decide, in a fully automated manner, what to buy and what to sell. There are over a hundred highly qualified people, many of them from IITs and IIMs, who have built all this capability.

My parents, my sister's and brother's families and several friends have invested in my firm's products. They are not financial experts, so they rely on my firm to help them invest well. I don't think they fully understand the investment products; they use them because they trust me as a person.

Similarly, most high net-worth investors (HNIs) have developed trust-based relationships with some expert or the other to help them invest properly. These experts have a good understanding of financial markets and the investors rely on their judgement. But this option is not available to an average investor. A professional with a reasonable amount of investment expertise and experience receives a remuneration of more than ₹1,000 an hour. Such a professional would charge at least ₹10–20,000 a year from an average investor. That is too high a cost for most of them. The average investor's portfolio size is less than ₹10,00,000. They can't afford to pay ₹10–20,000 for professional advice.

Take an example of a personal trainer. A personal trainer may charge ₹500 per session, so an average person may not be able to afford them. However, YouTube videos are an inexpensive alternative. Similarly, technology can change the cost dynamics of investment advice as well. So I set up a firm called Gulaq. Gulaq, or gullak, the piggy bank that many of us had as children, is a symbol of savings. In Gulaq, the objective was to simplify and automate the process of savings and investment to a level that any investor could afford to receive the benefit of expert advice.

This book is a description of such an investment process. Simple, easy to implement and likely to work reasonably well. 'Likely to work' does not mean that you will always have profits. Market investments are always subject to market risk and investors may lose money. The process works to position your investments in a manner that is appropriate for your situation.

This book is independent of Gulaq, the company. Once the reader understands the investment principles, they can implement their investment plan themselves, without using Gulaq, the company.

Acknowledgements

SELDOM HAS A SINGLE brain been able to produce a book. Especially a book like this, filled with definitions, examples and data. I have been helped by my colleagues at Estee and Gulaq in refining my thoughts and collecting information which has been used in this book.

Vivek Sharma, vice president of investments at Gulaq, was the prime collaborator. At one point, we discussed whether he or I should write this book. Vivek assigned me the task.

Abhirup Sen, Ramakrishna Bhimana and Simran worked closely on the book and collected and double checked the data and graphs. Nandan, our graphic designer, helped to create the charts.

My publisher, Bloomsbury, has been a wonderful partner. Krishan Chopra and Nitin Valecha gave me the confidence that the book was in good hands. Sanjiv Sarin provided the much-needed detailed editorial review, cleaning and polishing of both the concepts and the language. The book is much better with their efforts. Remaining errors, if any, are solely mine.

Introduction

MANY PEOPLE HAVE BEEN bitten by the stock market bug. Witness the rapid growth in trading accounts at online discount brokers. But only 11% of the individual stock traders made profits in trading according to a report published by SEBI in January 2023. They were the most active traders in the market. They were also investing in more advanced segments of the market, namely, futures and options.

Good investing is like good (i.e., healthy) eating, without getting tempted by fads. Everyone wants to do it, but almost no one can sustain a lifelong discipline. Tempting YouTube videos and strategically placed advertisements and articles constantly lure us to the latest diets. But the weight does not seem to budge. We are all looking for that superfood or super diet that will make us slim and fit. In our hearts, we know that good eating is about sticking to the basics—eat moderately, don't consume too much fat or sugar, balance macronutrients and drink enough water. But the lure of the latest fad diet is too much to resist. Some of us start on the journey with a decent plan but, along the way, we make mistakes which overwhelm the results.

> Chanchal (our fictional friend, no relation to any real Chanchal) plans to follow a diet. He[1] starts the morning with zeera and methi water. Then he does a 30-minute walk, before having fruits for breakfast. Lunch is just two

rotis with green vegetables and daal. Evening snack is a healthy plate of poha. Dinner is a clear soup and then some khichadi. But as the evening progresses, his stomach starts growling, and he pulls out a bag of chips. Then he makes himself a nice drink of whisky-and-soda and sits down to watch TV as he finishes the whole bag of chips. Not satisfied, he grabs an ice cream tub from the freezer. And so goes the day, well begun, but all undone by the end.

Chanchal approaches investments in a similar manner—with the conviction of a leaf blowing in the wind. He has very few role models. His parents keep their money in a bank—in a savings or a fixed deposit account or a PPF (Public Provident Fund) account. The bulk is invested in real estate.

As he starts to learn about stock market investments, the temptation of outsized returns overwhelms prudence. The anecdotes from his bragging friends are just too seductive. He starts to research the market and invests in some well-known companies and mutual funds. But the returns are not satisfying at all. Everyone else seems to be making a lot more money than him. So he buys shares of a small-cap company on a tip in a WhatsApp group of his class fellows. When the company does not perform well, he tries to make up by buying index options—they appear to be free money.

Thus, a well-intended plan of buying stocks of good companies and mutual funds deteriorates into a hodgepodge of risky investments. As markets turn, which they always do, the losses mount and inflict a big emotional damage on Chanchal. He liquidates his whole portfolio, incurring huge losses and vows to keep his money only in fixed deposits. Another good plan, well begun, but horribly ended.

The problem of finding good investments is not a lack of information; the problem is too much information. It is not that we do not know what healthy or unhealthy food is. The problem is of controlling our emotions while we follow the right path. And to avoid following the fad of the moment in the hope of making a quick gain. In the absence of a strong conviction in our plan, we run from one investment tip to another, from one obscure fragment of investment idea to another. Till we get overwhelmed by poor results and sell everything to put our money back in a fixed deposit, or worse, in a savings account.

This is where this book will be helpful. It will lay out a framework for developing a simple yet effective plan for growing your savings over your lifetime.

I have organized the book into four parts. The first part describes the components of a simple, systematic, investment plan, with examples about how to develop these components.

The second part will help cut through the noise that surrounds the subject of investment. Once you recognize what is noise, you will save time by ignoring what does not work.

The third part of the book contains the tools and information to keep working on the plan. Tools which will help you understand how to measure performance, rebalance your investments and optimize tax.

The fourth section is more technical, meant for those who would like more details.

I have tried to keep the core message of the book simple and brief. The basic principles of investing do not change quickly. They have been consistent for several decades, ever since the concepts of investment management were articulated in the middle of the twentieth century.

However, the information accompanying the principles, that is, the details of the products and their management, changes all the time. Hence it cannot be covered in a book like this which has a fixed format. This information is available on the companion website at gulaq.com.

Part 1

Building an Investment Plan

Setting Expectations

We always overestimate the change that will occur in the next two years and underestimate the change that will occur in the next ten.

—Bill Gates

THE FIRST STEP IN building a good plan is knowing what a good plan is. The world used to be a simple place when everyone invested in a fixed deposit and received the same return as everyone else. But now, when we move to the capricious world of stock markets, our expectations are set by the returns we hear everyone else is getting. The problem is that people share only the good stories—the stock that they bought which tripled in a month. We never hear about the cases where they lost money. So how do we know what to expect from our investments?

There are two main types of investments—equity and debt. Equity refers to the investments in stocks, where the returns are variable, and debt is where the rate of return is fixed at the time of investment itself. Let us look at what kinds of returns these two main sources of investments have given over the past 40 years.

In equity, the track record of Sensex is shown in Figure 1.1. When we look at it annually, the return varies between 82.1% and -52.5%. When we see it on a rolling[2] 5-year basis, it varies between 43.1% and –1.8%. And when we see the rolling

10-year return, then it varies between 23.5% and 2.6%. The average return is 17.8%. We take rolling returns to evaluate all possible scenarios. For example, if we were to look at returns from 2010 to 2020 and we only saw returns from 1 January to 31 December every year, we will get one set of figures. But it is possible that the highest 12-month return happened from 1 May to 30 April of the next year. That is why we use rolling returns which take all possible 12-month periods to estimate the maximum and minimum returns.

> Averages tell only a part of the picture, whereas maximum and minimum figures indicate the range of risk you are exposed to. Will you cross a river that is 4 feet deep, on an average? While this might seem safe at first glance, it is important to consider that the maximum depth could be anything—even 20 feet. Ignoring the maximum depth could lead to dangerous situations. In investments, it is important to consider extremes rather than relying solely on averages for decision making.

Another thing to observe is that the return varies a lot from year to year. For rolling 10 years, it varies a lot less. So it is much easier to predict the return over the next 10 years compared to predicting the return for the next 1 year.

FIGURE 1.1 Sensex Returns

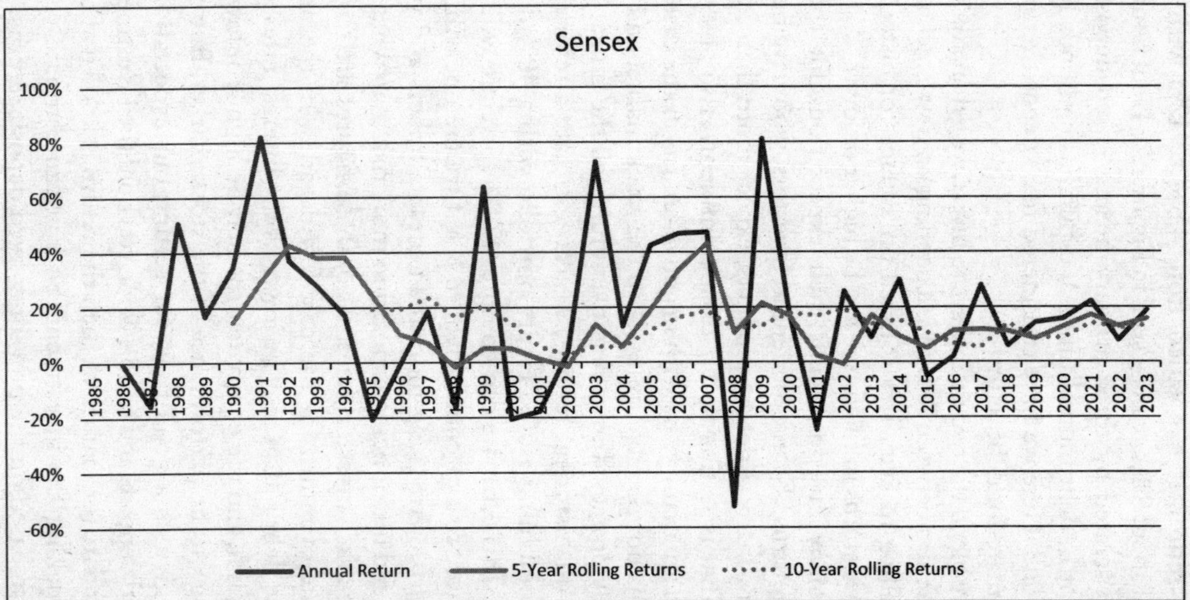

For debt return, it has varied from 4.6% to 12% with an average of about 8%, as can be seen in Figure 1.2.[3] Debt returns can be generated by three primary means—fixed deposits, investment in debt mutual funds and purchasing bonds like Bharat Bond. Here we have considered fixed deposit returns as an estimate for debt returns.

So, if we blend the two main ways to invest, we get an average expected return between 8–17.8% depending on how much risk we are willing to take. This is based on averages of historical return. The returns in the future can be higher or lower.

How many investors tailor their expectations for these levels of returns? Even experienced investors, who have been exposed to many different products, expect more than 20% returns. That is setting up for disappointment. Also observe that there are many years with negative returns in the case of equity. It is not possible to invest in the stock market and be completely protected from negative returns all the time.

Based on historical returns, we can estimate a return of 14% by combining a 60% equity portfolio with a 40% debt portfolio. This estimate can go up to 17.8% if we are willing to take more risk or come down to 8% if we are not willing to accept risk. Anything more than these numbers and you are being fed lies or being exposed to more risk than what an average market investor faces. Also, these figures are based on the rate of return for the past few decades. In the near future, the debt return may be lower as the interest rates are not that high, and the equity returns may be higher or lower, depending on the performance of the stock market. But the averages give us a good basis for setting our expectations. With fixed deposits and bonds, when you hold the investment till its due date (or maturity), then the return is known at the time of making the investment. So you can estimate your total return based on the prevailing fixed deposit returns.

Power of Compounding

Compound interest is the eighth wonder of the world.

—Albert Einstein

IF YOU FEEL DISCOURAGED after reading the previous section, 'Setting Expectations', it is perhaps because you may not fully understand the power of compounding. If you compounded your money at 12% a year, how much would you have after 40 years—4x? 8x? 12x? 20x? Guess again—it is 93x! For each rupee invested and compounded at 12% every year, you will have 93 rupees after 40 years.

I mentioned in the previous chapter that, historically, conservative investing earned 8% return and aggressive investing earned about 17.8% return. Table 1.1 shows the power of compounding.

TABLE 1.1 Power of Compounding

		Years Invested			
		10	20	30	40
Growth Rate	8%	2.2	4.7	10.1	21.7
	12%	3.1	9.6	30	93.1
	16%	4.4	19.5	85.8	378.7
	20%	6.2	38.3	237.4	1,469.8

Take the case of an investor who invested a sum of money for 40 years. If he invested conservatively, he would earn 21.7x, if he invested aggressively (and earned 16% average), he would earn 378.7x. That is 17 times more money.

The longer the period of investment, the stronger is the power of compounding. Let us look at another example.

> Chanchal Kumar plans to save ₹10,000 a month for his retirement. Let's say he starts at the age of 55 and saves till his retirement, which is at the age of 65. Also assume his savings grow at the rate of 10% per annum. At the time of retirement, he will have a corpus of about ₹20 lakh. If he started 10 years earlier and saved for 20 years, how much more money will he have? Double? No. He will have ₹75 lakh—more than 3 times the amount. Table 1.2 shows how the money multiplies faster as the saving period increases.

TABLE 1.2 Early Investing

Investment per month (₹)	10,000
Saved till retirement age	65
Expected return	10%
Start Saving at Age	**Final Savings (₹)**
25	6,32,41,000
35	2,26,05,000
45	75,94,000
55	20,48,000

The impact of this will be even more stark if the rate of return was higher. In Table 1.3, we see a comparison between growth at a rate of return at 10% versus a rate of return at 15%.

TABLE 1.3 Impact of Rate of Return

	Expected Return	
Age	10%	15%
25	6,32,41,000	31,01,61,000
35	2,26,05,000	6,92,33,000
45	75,94,000	1,49,72,000
55	20,48,000	27,52,000

Check Your Understanding

1. If you invest ₹1 at 12% interest for 40 years, how much will you have at the end of the investment period?
   a. ₹3.1
   b. ₹9.6
   c. ₹30.0
   d. ₹93.1
2. If you invest ₹10,000 per month for 20 years at 10% interest, how much money will you have at the end of the investment period?
   a. ₹20 lakh
   b. ₹40 lakh
   c. ₹75 lakh
   d. ₹1 crore
3. If Chanchal Kumar starts saving for his retirement at the age of 45 instead of 55, how much more money will he have at the time of his retirement? (assuming 15% return)
   a. ₹50 lakh
   b. ₹1 crore
   c. ₹1.2 crore
   d. ₹2 crore

4. If Parvat Kumar invests ₹10,000 per month for 40 years at 10% interest and Chanchal Kumar invests ₹20,000 per month for 20 years, also at 10% interest, who will have more money?
   a. Parvat Kumar will have more as he is investing for longer
   b. Chanchal Kumar will have more as he is investing more per month
   c. Both will have the same amount, as one is investing double the amount and the other is investing for double the time

Answers: 1–d, 2–c, 3–b, 4–a

Start with a Simple Plan

THE SIMPLEST FORM OF investment is a fixed deposit. You earn a known return every year. There are other fixed return or 'debt' products which we have discussed in the section 'Setting Expectations'. That is the best you can do if you can't or don't want to take any risk. To have a chance of earning a higher return, you would need to take a little risk—risk means higher variability in the return. If you take more risk, you may earn more on an average, but sometimes you will earn less. If you can accept that, then your investment can include a broad stock market investment instrument. The simplest instrument to do this is an index fund. We will talk more about index funds later.

So a combination of a debt and an index fund can meet the investment needs of nearly all investors except the very large ones or special cases. The most common version of this combination is to invest 60% of the funds available in equity markets and 40% in debt products. This is called a '60–40' portfolio. It is simple to implement. The return from this portfolio should serve as your benchmark return.

As shown in Table 1.4, in the benchmark allocation of 60% equity and 40% debt, the rolling average return is 13.37%. During the period, 6 out of 33 years had a negative return with a maximum loss of 32.71% for a 12-month rolling return. If you are like most people, you will not be willing to lose 33%

TABLE 1.4 Returns of a Model Portfolio

Debt Allocation	40%
Equity Allocation	60%
Years with Negative Return (1991–2023)	18%
Maximum Loss (MDD)	–28.58%
Rolling 12-month Average Return	13.37%
Best 12-month Rolling Return	136.49%
Worst 12-month Rolling Return	–32.71%

of your money. However, that is the risk of investing in equity markets. In the short term, they can produce significant losses. The only way to reduce the possibility of a loss is to gravitate towards fixed return investments. This also sacrifices some returns. Remember the maxim, 'No risk, no return'.

Side Bar: Benchmark

A benchmark is a standard for comparison. The original use of the term was when marks used to be made on a stone pillar to measure the level of water in a river or the height of an ocean tide. In investing, benchmark means a comparison used to evaluate the performance of an investment. It is not wise to compare returns of a fixed deposit with an investment in the stock market—the two carry different risks and hence are not comparable. The benchmark for fixed deposits is the average fixed deposit rate published by the Reserve Bank of India (RBI).[5] A benchmark for investments in stock market is the return of a broad market index, like the Nifty 50 or Sensex.

A benchmark can be set for each part of the asset allocation—debt and equity investment and also for specialized allocations like small caps or a sector fund. When you combine the benchmarks of each allocation area with the weights in the portfolio, you get the benchmark for the overall portfolio.

Check Your Understanding

1. What is the model portfolio?
   a. 60% in equities and 40% in debt
   b. 40% in equities and 60% in debt
   c. 50% in equities and 50% in debt
   d. 40% in equities, 40% in debt, 20% in cash
2. What returns are a sign of the skill of the investor in the stock market?
   a. Positive returns
   b. Returns more than 20%
   c. Returns in excess of benchmark returns
   d. Returns more than fixed deposit rates
3. What is the benchmark for the model portfolio?
   a. Fixed deposit rate
   b. Nifty returns
   c. A combination of Nifty returns and fixed deposit returns in the model ratio

Answers: 1–a, 2–c, 3–c

Assessing Goals

This is a story of someone I know—Rajat. He is 30 years old and recently married. The couple is expecting their first child in 4 months. Rajat earns ₹12 lakh a year and lives with his parents. He wants to move out into an independent apartment. He recently bought a new car. The car was a little more expensive than he was comfortable with, but he managed to get a car loan from his bank.

What do you see as a suitable investment and savings plan for Rajat? He is living beyond his current means and adding to his obligations (new baby, larger home, car loan payment).

MANY PEOPLE SUFFER FROM reckless overconfidence when it comes to assessment of financial goals. They under-save and spend way beyond their capacity to sustain their expenses. As a result, they fall short of money for their requirements later in life. Either they don't think at all or have overconfidence in their ability to increase their earnings as their spending increases. They don't factor in increased requirements when their children are born—they will need to be educated, fed and housed. Very seldom do they factor in savings for their retirement. It seems so far away that it becomes irrelevant.

Estimating Your Savings Requirements

Everyone wants more. But how much is enough? You need to have a good estimate of your savings requirements to feel good about your savings plan. A common topic among young professionals is the amount of money that they need to have in their bank account so that they can have peace of mind. Let us term this as 'Peace of Mind Money'—the amount of money which, if you had it, would give you confidence to do what you want with your earnings without the need to save any more. This is a good way to think about the savings requirement for retirement and other major goals. Very few people—the ones who were born into rich families—have Peace of Mind Money. And no one—including the very rich—know the amount of Peace of Mind Money they need. How does a person estimate Peace of Mind Money?

To get an idea, let us discuss three big financial goals in detail. These are retirement, home purchase and children's education.

Retirement

The savings goal for retirement is to cover the living expenses in the years when you are no longer earning a regular income. Then you need to rely totally on your savings to fund your living expenses. To calculate your retirement money, you need to estimate your living expenses per year and the number of years of retirement. In the next section, we will discuss a simple template to estimate annual living expenses. If you get a good estimate of your living expenses for a couple of years, then you can use that to estimate what you would need over your life, using estimates for inflation (i.e., how costs will go up over time). We will assume that till retirement age, you will be earning enough every year to meet your living expenses and put away some savings for your retirement and other goals.

So the goal of retirement savings will only be to meet the living expenses once you have retired. This is likely to be the largest savings goal you will have. You may have other savings goals too, like buying a house or going on a holiday. And if you are one of the few who will receive a lifelong pension, then your calculations need to be adjusted for that.

Also, many people rely on their children as a form of retirement savings. They invest in their children's education and upbringing and expect that the children will bear their living expenses later. You should assess what the family expectations are in your situation and whether you would rely on your children or your own savings to pay a part or all of your expenses on retirement.

In some cases, you may own a farm or a small business and plan to rely on the income from there to pay for your living expenses. In this case, there is no fixed retirement date. But even then, a retirement savings plan is still a good idea for two reasons. One reason is that at some point you will stop working for the business full-time. At that time, if some other family members are running the business, you will have to share the earnings with them. So you cannot assume that all the earnings will be available to fund your personal expenses. The second reason is to realize that the business will continue to generate income even after you pass away. This future earning potential beyond your life time can be converted into money for use in your retirement. For example, you may own a shop from which you receive a monthly rent. This is your passive income and it will continue till you sell the asset. You may not be able to sustain your expenses only on the rental income, but if you consider the sale value of the property, you may be able to fund your retirement. Also, if you are planning to pass on the asset to the next generation, then you can expect some support for your retirement expenses from the earnings of your children. If you do not have to leave the asset for the next generation, then you could borrow against the property and spend that money to support your living expenses. This is called 'reverse mortgage'. Many banks offer products in which, against the pledge of an asset like property, you receive a payout every month. All these amounts keep getting accumulated as a loan. The total debt is then paid off by selling off your property after your death and the excess money, if any, from the sale is paid to your successors.

The annual living expenses till retirement would need to be adjusted for changes like the needs of young children (they will eventually grow up and earn their own income), requirements of ageing parents and payments towards loans. These requirements are there for different time periods at different stages of the life of an individual.

After all adjustments, you may estimate that your current monthly expense requirement is, for example, ₹50,000 or ₹1,00,000. That becomes your baseline. Over time, the expenses may increase due to inflation, but at the same time, the investment amount will also grow. So to keep the calculations simple, we will assume that the investment growth will compensate for inflation. As an organization, at Gulaq we provide a more precise template to calculate your savings requirements where you can select an investment growth that is different from the inflation rate. But let us keep things simple for the time being to understand the basic concepts first.

After estimating the baseline expenses, the next part is a tough question. Here you need to face your own mortality. No one wants to think about it, but it is an essential requirement for retirement planning. For how many years would you require the retirement income? In the year 2023, in India, an average person could expect to live till 70 years. This is the average for all people, including young people. As you grow older, life expectancy also keeps increasing. So a 60-year-old person can expect to live till 80 years. Depending on your health and family history, you should pick an estimate of how long you would be living in retirement.

Many people have a fear of running out of retirement money if they live longer than average. This can be addressed by an investment product like an annuity which combines the properties of an investment and insurance. In the case of a life annuity, the insurance company pays a constant amount of money over the lifespan of the investor. This amount can also increase over time at a pre-agreed rate to take care of inflation—of course, at an extra cost.

Putting this all together, say, you retire at the age of 65 and expect to live till 80. This would mean that you require ₹50,000 a month for 15 years of your retirement. So, you require ₹90 lakh of savings (50,000 x 12 x 15) today to have enough money for retirement.

Children's Education

Children's education is becoming more expensive every year. Various estimates of education inflation are 5–8% depending on the brand value of the educational institution. Also, our expectations of the type of education we want for our children is increasing. Many parents who studied in government schools and colleges in India wish to educate their children in international schools or in foreign universities. Again, we will assume that on a blended basis, the growth in investment will pay for the inflation in costs. So, you need to find the current cost of education in the school and college you expect to send your children to. Depending on the type of institution, the fees can vary widely, by as much as a factor of 100 (Figure 1.3). An education in government institutions may cost only ₹1 lakh for 16 years of school and college education. A private school education could cost ₹30 lakh. A professional degree could cost around ₹20 lakh. And if you plan to send your children abroad for college, then the cost skyrockets to over ₹1.5 crore per child.

FIGURE 1.3 Cost of Education

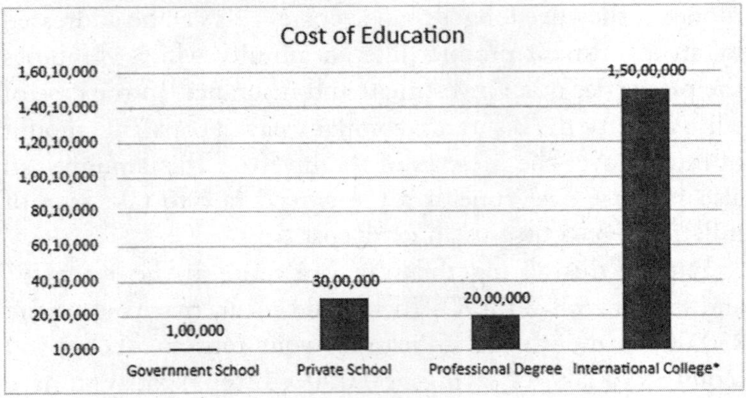

Assuming two children and the prevailing cost of private school and professional college education, you need to have ₹1 crore to meet the children's education goals.

Buying a Home

Another big savings goal for many people is buying a house. There are a few considerations around the loan you will be able to get to buy your house. Usually, you can get a loan of up to 80% of the value of the house. This reduces the savings goal to a smaller amount, say 20%, of the buying price. On the other hand, it reduces the savings potential in the subsequent years as you will have to pay the EMI (equated monthly instalments) every month as repayment of the loan. There are a lot of online loan payment calculators which help you assess what you can expect as your EMI. In India, usually the rent of the property is less than the interest cost, so your rental payment may not cover the EMI or the loan repayment amount.

The term of the loan (i.e., the loan period), besides the size of the loan, has an impact on the monthly payment. The longer the duration of the loan, the lower would be the EMI. Some banks in India have started to offer 30-year home loans to their preferred customers, who work in some large companies.

As a starting point, you should estimate the loan amount you can take by comparing the EMI with your rent payout. Let us say that you want to buy a house for ₹60 lakh. Then you would need to have ₹12 lakh for the down payment as the bank will usually give only 80% of the price of the property as loan.

Table 1.5 lists down the amounts we have discussed so far.

TABLE 1.5 Assessing Goals

Goal	Amount Required (₹)
Retirement	90,00,000
Children's Education	1,00,00,000
Buying a House (down payment)	12,00,000
Total Savings Required	2,02,00,000

Putting the three goals together—retirement, children's education and buying a house—you need ₹202 lakh as Peace of Mind Money.

If you don't have this much money, you should start using a disciplined monthly savings plan. Again, to simplify the calculations, divide the Peace of Mind Money by the number of months of savings before retirement. So, if you are 30 years old and think you will work till the age of 65, then divide ₹202 lakh by 420. Thus, you need to save ₹48,000 every month. This is an approximation, just to illustrate what we are discussing. The accurate amount would have to be adjusted for inflation rate, income and savings growth rate, expected investment returns and timing of the various goals and expenses. As a first order estimate, this will be a good approximation.

To save this amount may appear to be a daunting task. The amount can be modified by changing some of the assumptions. Like planning to work longer and having a shorter retirement period. Or adjusting other requirements around investment in a house or expenditure in retirement.

There is also a trend among young people to figure out an early retirement plan—the FIRE or Financial Independence, Retire Early movement. To calculate your FIRE money, you need to take your Peace of Mind Money and add your monthly living expenses till anticipated retirement. In our example, that is ₹50,000 a month for 30 years. That is ₹1,80,00,000. So by adding this amount to the Peace of Mind Money, you can get your FIRE money estimate.

This is obviously a large amount even after assuming that you would not be expanding your lifestyle expenses.

Foreign Vacation and Other Goals

Many people have very specific goals like saving for a vacation or even buying an iPhone. Should you be saving separately for such goals? Such goals are more a lifestyle expense than a financial goal. A rule of thumb might be to not keep a separate financial goal for anything which requires less than 10% of your annual income.

> There is a story of a professor who taught the importance of focussing on what is important in a vivid manner.
>
> He brought a big glass jar to the class and a bag full of some things. First, he pulled out big rocks and filled up the jar. He asked his students, if they thought the jar was full. And they all said, yes, it was full. Then the professor took out some marbles and started dropping them into the jar. The marbles found the empty spaces between the rocks. The professor asked again if the students thought that the jar was full. The students said yes, now it was full.

The professor then pulled out a bag of sand and dropped some sand into the jar. The sand filled all the gaps between the rocks and the marbles. The professor asked again if the students thought the jar was full. The students were amused and said that the professor had tricked them, but they were quite sure that the jar was full. At that point, the professor pulled out a bottle of water and poured it into the jar. The water easily seeped into the sand. The professor then explained, 'The big rocks are the important things in life. First fill your time with them. This is your family, your own health and your main livelihood. The marbles are your smaller objectives but still important. These are your friends, your hobbies and passions. The sand represents the day-to-day activities and the water represents entertainment and other activities we can fill our time with. If we start with pouring sand and water in the jar first, there will be no place for the marbles or rocks. You must first fit the important things in life.'

Savings are the same. You must plan for the big events in your life—retirement, home and children's education. These are the rocks. Vacations, big purchases are important, but they are like marbles and come after you have filled your jar with the rocks. And spending on a party or a dinner at a restaurant is the sand. You should only fill it in the space that is left after you have taken care of the rocks and marbles. Water represents entertainment and impulse buys. It should only fit in after all other needs have been met.

Estimating Annual Spend and Savings Capacity

Estimating your savings capability requires you to have a good sense of your annual expenses. A diligent person, with access to all his bank statements and after spending several days, can arrive at a good estimate of his annual expense. This book is not meant to teach you how to create an expense budget. There are many detailed budgeting and expense planning apps available which you can use.

To get a working estimate of your expenses, we have a simple template which can be completed by most people in a couple of hours.

The core idea of the template is to focus on the net spending instead of getting into a granular breakup of each type of spending. The problem of having a granular tally of expenses is that it requires meticulous record-keeping and the amount of work needed to be done is large. To create an estimate of your annual expenditure, you can use a simpler method of seeing how much you spend month by month. This can be calculated at the bank account level. The total change in bank account is caused by money-in, by large purchase or the sale of assets and by expenses.

Money-in is the income you earn. This includes your salary, business income, rentals or any other source of income. Other sources could be gifts, dividends, etc. You have to be careful about adjusting large asset transactions that are not regular expenses. You may have bought something expensive (like a gold coin) or sold something expensive (like a flat). This money is neither an income nor an expense. It is changing one asset for another. In this case, cash into a gold coin or a flat into cash.

Once you have adjusted for large asset transactions, all the reduction in bank account is an expense. The process is explained in further detail in the Appendix 'Estimating Annual Spend'.

If your income is greater than your spending, then you have savings. The average savings rate in India in March 2022 was about 30%. It has been coming down over the years. A decade earlier, in 2011, the savings rate was about 36%. So, if the savings potential you have estimated in this exercise comes out to be 25–40%, then you are well within the normal range. If it is lower, then you should think whether you have higher than normal expenses for a good reason—maybe you are supporting your extended family or you have extra expenses right now, like paying for the college education of your children.

Understanding the Time Period of Your Investments

Another factor in your savings plan is understanding when you will need the money. This is called the 'liquidity need'. Liquidity means the ability to convert an investment into spendable cash. If you own a farm far away from the town in a remote part of the country, it might not be easy to sell it. If you can't sell it easily, it can't be converted into spendable cash easily. The other factor in understanding the liquidity need is the impact of cashing investments when they are at a low value.

The most startling example to help understand the liquidity need is the hedge fund called Long Term Capital Management (LTCM) and its unravelling in 1998. LTCM was the shining star of the financial world during most of the 1990s. Nobel laureates like Myron Scholes and Robert Merton (of the Black-Scholes-Merton option pricing model fame) were principals in the firm. The fund made outsized profits for several years. But in 1998, as Russia went through a default, their portfolio lost money. Not only did they lose money, there were simply no buyers for the securities they were holding, that is, they had a liquidity problem. All the experts agreed that their losses were temporary and they would be able to recover them, but at that time, as they lost more and more money and could not sell their securities to cover their losses, LTCM had to be sold off to a consortium of 14 banks. The owners of the fund—some of the smartest investors in the world—lost billions of dollars in the fire sale.

So even the most sophisticated investors in the world can be caught unawares due to the liquidity risk. How does an average investor protect their savings plan against this risk? How do you ensure you will have spendable cash when you actually need it?

We will have more to say about this in the section 'Refining Your Investment Style'.

Check Your Understanding

1. What is the first step to estimating retirement money?
   a. Estimate your living expenses per year
   b. Estimate the cost of children's education
   c. Estimate the cost of a new car
   d. Estimate the cost of health insurance
2. What is the goal of retirement savings?
   a. To cover the cost of living while you are earning a salary
   b. To cover the cost of living after retirement when you are no longer earning an income
   c. To pay for expensive vacations after retirement
3. Which of the following is *not* one of the three big goals covered in this chapter?
   a. Retirement
   b. Children's education
   c. Health insurance
   d. Home purchase
4. What is the average life expectancy in India?
   a. 60 years
   b. 70 years
   c. 80 years

Answers: 1–a, 2–b, 3–c, 4–b

Refining Your Investment Style

Risk Tolerance

Risk is a concept that is not well understood by an average investor. Most people view risk as the risk of loss of principal. In the world of investments, risk is usually measured by uncertainty.

> Chanchal Kumar, our friend, has two friends. Parvat Kumar is very reliable. If you make a plan with him, you can be sure that he will remember and follow through. But Nazuk Singh is full of contradictions. Sometimes he is very active and a lot of fun; at other times, he is not interested in doing anything at all. You can plan all you want, but you will not know how Nazuk would act on the planned day. This uncertainty of behaviour is 'risk'. Parvat Kumar is dependable, though a little boring. Nazuk is a lot more fun but also unpredictable.

Investments are also like this. Some investments are dependable, though they provide lower returns. For example, fixed deposits. Other investments can provide much higher profits, like stocks, but the returns are uncertain. This uncertainty is the risk.

How much risk you can take depends on two main factors. First, and more important, is your mental makeup and attitude. Some people are okay with uncertainty and may even seek the thrill that it provides. Others become uncomfortable and need certainty.

The second factor is the safety margin. The longer the goal and higher the savings relative to your needs, more can be the uncertainty that you can handle. That is, you can work at a lower safety margin.

Let me explain this with an example from everyday life. Some people drive fast and others drive very carefully. How people drive can be explained by two factors—one is their personality and the other is the driving conditions. Let us consider personality. Some people are comfortable driving fast and do not feel the stress of remaining fully alert with split-second reactions. Others are cautious and want time to react to any event on the road. This has nothing to do with the car or the road conditions, but only the personality and comfort level of the individual.

The other factor is the driving conditions. Even the most speed-loving driver will adjust their speed for weather and road conditions. If you are driving at night during a spell of heavy rain, you will drive slowly; if the weather is pleasant and the roads are open and clear, you will drive faster.

Similarly, in investments you need to assess your investment situation. If you need money soon or the money you have is just enough for your needs, you should not take much risk with it. You should invest in fixed return options. If the goals are a long time away or you expect growth in your savings capability, you can take more risk. So younger people can take more risks than older people who are near retirement. Your situation with your savings level, earning potential, age and safety buffer will determine your investment allocations. It is equally important to know what not to take into consideration while deciding your investments. Don't focus too much on market conditions. This is called 'market timing' and we will discuss it in detail later. Market timing is treacherously difficult to assess and certainly not something that a regular investor should be doing on their own.

Thus, your risk tolerance is a combination of your personality, your savings capability and the time available before you need the savings.

TABLE 1.6 Risk and Return of Gears

	Gear 1	Gear 2	Gear 3	Gear 4	Gear 5	Gear 6
Debt Allocation	100%	80%	60%	40%	20%	0%
Equity Allocation	0%	20%	40%	60%	80%	100%
Negative Return Years	0	1	6	6	7	9
Maximum Loss (MDD)	0.0%	-6.0%	-20.0%	-32.2%	-43.0%	-53.0%
Average Returns (1 Year)	7.9%	9.0%	10.3%	11.6%	13.0%	14.3%
Best Year Returns	12.7%	19.8%	33.7%	48.6%	64.4%	86.2%
Worst Year Returns	4.7%	-6.4%	-20.0%	-32.2%	-43.0%	-53.0%
Average 12-month Rolling Returns	7.9%	9.0%	10.3%	11.5%	12.8%	14.1%
Best 12-month Rolling Returns	12.7%	21.4%	37.3%	54.9%	74.3%	95.7%
Worst 12-month Rolling Returns	4.7%	-6.7%	-20.4%	-32.7%	-43.5%	-53.0%
Probability of Postive Returns in 12 months	100.0%	96.6%	79.3%	79.3%	75.9%	69.0%

One easy method, taking the driving analogy further, is to use investment 'Gears'. If your risk tolerance is low, then use a low Gear. If it is high, then use a higher Gear. The different Gears represent varying levels of equity and debt investments. Gear 1 is all fixed income—low risk, low return and low variability. Gear 6 is all equity—higher risk, higher return and higher variability. In Table 1.6, we have laid out the investment outcome range for various Gears. As you can see, higher the Gear, higher the return—but also, higher the variability in outcomes. So uncertainty and returns go hand-in-hand.

It is not easy to know your risk tolerance. Often, we feel we can take a lot of risk but the panic that sets in when we are faced with losses is all-consuming. There are others who are so conservative that they never invest in anything other than fixed deposits in banks. Emotionally and financially, they may not be able to handle market movements calmly.

Side Bar: Risk Assessment Tool

Many advisors ask potential investors some questions to help assess their risk tolerance. Take this quiz to determine your risk score. There is a detailed online version of this quiz available at https://www.gulaq.com/risk-calculator/.

1. I plan to begin withdrawing money from my investments in:
   a. Less than 3 years (1)
   b. 3–5 years (4)
   c. 6–10 years (10)
   d. More than 10 years (14)
2. My savings are meant to support my lifestyle in retirement. I plan to spend my savings in:
   a. Less than 2 years (0)
   b. 2–5 years (1)
   c. 6–10 years (6)
   d. More than 10 years (11)
3. Currently, my income sources (such as salary, business income, rental, pension, etc.) are:
   a. Very unstable (0)
   b. Unstable (3)
   c. Somewhat stable (6)
   d. Stable (9)
   e. Very stable (11)

4. My experience with the following products is (select all that apply):
    a. Mutual Funds
        i. None (0)
        ii. Some (3)
        iii. Extensive (6)
    b. Individual Stocks
        i. None (0)
        ii. Some (4)
        iii. Extensive (9)
    c. Futures and Options
        i. None (0)
        ii. Some (6)
        iii. Extensive (11)
5. When I invest my money, I am:
    a. Most concerned about my investment losing value (0)
    b. Equally concerned about my investment losing or gaining value (6)
    c. Most concerned about my investment gaining value (11)
6. Imagine that in the past 3 months, the equity market lost 25% of its value. An individual stock you own also lost 25% of its value. What would you do?
    a. Sell the entire stock (0)
    b. Sell some of the stock (3)
    c. Do nothing (7)
    d. Buy more stock (11)

7. Review the following scenarios. We've outlined the most-likely, best-case and worst-case annual returns of five hypothetical investment plans. Which range of possible outcomes is most acceptable to you?
   a. Plan A: Average 8.2%, Best case 10.2%, Worst case 5.5% (0)
   b. Plan B: Average 9.3%, Best case 18.8%, Worst case 1.9% (4)
   c. Plan C: Average 11.1%, Best case 43%, Worst case –14.3% (9)
   d. Plan D: Average 13.6%, Best case 76.7%, Worst case –35.7% (11)
   e. Plan E: Average 15.7%, Best case 98.9%, Worst case –41.7% (16)

Scoring Metrics

Gear	Score
2	1–20
3	21–40
4	41–60
5	61–80
6	81–100

Liquidity Needs

Let's say our friend Chanchal Kumar has saved ₹9 lakh. He expects to buy a home in 3 years and would require ₹10 lakh as down payment on the home. How should he assess the impact of this liquidity need on his savings plan?

In Table 1.7, you can see that investment in Gear 1 will meet the requirement of investing ₹10 lakh for 3 years in both best- and worst-case outcome. However, the investment in Gear 2, Gear 3, Gear 4, Gear 5 or Gear 6 will carry some risk. In the worst-case scenario, the total amount will be less than ₹10 lakh and Chanchal Kumar will run the risk of not meeting his goal. While higher Gears allow you to earn higher returns, they also introduce the risk of falling short of your goals.

Now, let's change the scenario just a little bit. Let's say Chanchal Kumar needed only ₹8 lakh as down payment on the house. In this case, even investment in Gear 3 will meet the liquidity needs. So Chanchal Kumar can take a little more risk with the investments as the additional return, if it happens, will mean larger savings at the end of 3 years.

The right level of risk for you would depend on the timing of your goals (that is, liquidity needs) and the amount of savings available to meet those goals. If you have very large savings compared to your needs, then you can afford to take more risk, as the excess return will generate additional funds for you without increasing the chances of missing your goal. Figure 1.4 explains this pictorially.

TABLE 1.7 Best-Case and Worst-Case Outcomes for ₹10,00,000 investment

INR Lacs	Gear1	Gear2	Gear3	Gear4	Gear5	Gear6
Worst Outcome after 3 Years	10.47	9.78	8.53	7.39	6.36	5.43
Best Outcome after 3 Years	12.69	16.27	20.65	25.58	30.94	36.62

FIGURE 1.4 Adjusting Risk Levels

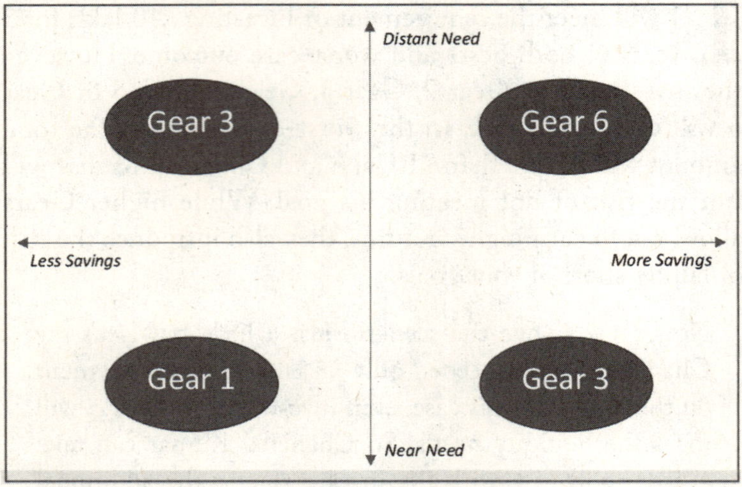

Business Investment and ESOPs

Many people have investments in a business they own. It could be a shop or a small agricultural farm or a franchise store. Or it could be that they have received employee stock options (ESOPs) in the company that they work in. How does a person evaluate investment in a business versus investment in other securities? Here are a few considerations:

1. Concentration risk: It is quite normal to keep reinvesting all your earnings into your business. I have been through this experience. I had built a company and sold it in 2006. As a part of the transaction, I received some cash and some shares. I really believed in the business, so with the cash I received, I bought some more shares in the same company. This was a very risky action on my part since I was concentrating all my risk in one company. In 2008, the stock market crashed and the company stock fell over 50%. So my entire investment was heavily impacted. The right strategy in 2006 would have been to use the cash to buy some other, uncorrelated investments.
2. Illiquidity: Also, for most small business owners, the investment in their own business is an illiquid investment. In case of requirement, they cannot encash their investment. I observed this with a close relative. They had a thriving business and kept reinvesting the profits into the business. In a particular year, due to some reasons, they were short of money to meet their obligations. In a pinch, their only option was to sell their house and move to a rented house. While they were asset rich, due to liquidity constraints, they ended up having limited choices to handle a sudden requirement for cash. Similarly, some private companies provide ESOPs as an incentive. While this is lucrative, it does increase the illiquidity risk. You have the assets but not the ability to convert them into cash immediately.

In some situations, this illiquidity can be resolved by borrowing against the assets from a bank. You should assess the possibility of doing so while assessing the illiquidity risk. In general, it is difficult to get loans against shares in a private company. Land, house, gold and similar tradable assets are easier to use as a security for loans. Even when you pledge a security, the bank will still assess your ability to repay the loan and interest.

3. Linkage with your employment earnings: When you invest in your business or you hold significant amount of your savings as ESOPs in the company you work in, your investment return is somewhat linked to your employment earnings. If the business or the company does well, then the value of your investment will also do well. At the same time, the salary or bonuses you earn from the company will also increase. But if the business does not do well, then it is double jeopardy—the value of investment will reduce and so will the income from the company, and in the worst case, it may even stop.

Check Your Understanding

1. Which of the following is a risk associated with investing in a business that you own?
   a. Concentration risk
   b. Illiquidity
   c. Both concentration risk and illiquidity
   d. Neither concentration risk nor illiquidity
2. Which of the following is not a risk associated with investing in employee stock options (ESOPs)?
   a. Concentration risk
   b. Illiquidity
   c. Your employment is linked to the performance of the company
   d. The value of your ESOPs can decline if the company does poorly

3. Which of the following is the best strategy for managing the risk of investing in a business that you own?
    a. Reinvest all your profits back into the business
    b. Invest your savings in opportunities not linked with your business
    c. Only invest money that you can afford to lose
    d. Both b and c

Answers: 1–c, 2–c, 3–b

Tax Considerations

TAXES CAN TAKE AWAY a significant chunk of your savings. They are the cost we pay to live in a civilized society. While taxes are unavoidable, they can be minimized legally. Tax rates are different for different types of investors, different types of investments and for different time periods of investments (Table 1.8). A lower tax is better than a higher tax, and tax that becomes due later is better than tax that becomes due now.

TABLE 1.8 Tax Rates (2023 Budget)

Asset	Short-Term	Long-Term
Equity (Domestic)	15% (< 1 year)	10% (> 1 year)
Equity (Foreign)	Regular Income Tax Slabs (<2 years)	20% with indexation (>2 years)
Interest from Fixed Income Instruments (FD, Bonds)	Regular Income Tax Slabs	
Real Estate	Regular Income Tax Slabs (<2 years)	20% with indexation (>2 years)

Chanchal Kumar, Manoj Kumar and Parvat Kumar are friends. Chanchal Kumar trades every month. Manoj Kumar trades after one year. Parvat Kumar is the slowest of the three and holds the same security for 10 years. How much difference will it make to their assets after 10 years?

The post-tax returns after 10 years, assuming that their investment yields 15% return a year and the transaction costs are 0.05%, are shown in Figure 1.5. Chanchal Kumar will grow his money from 100 to 331—a big gain indeed. But Manoj will grow his money to 353, 7% more than Chanchal. The best result will be with Parvat, who will grow his money to 374 (another 6% above Manoj). You may wonder why there is a difference between Manoj's and Parvat's returns as both of them are paying long-term capital gains tax of 10%. The difference is due to delaying the payment of tax from every year to the end of 10 years. Parvat gets to earn return on the part of tax that has not yet become due.

FIGURE 1.5 Tax Impact of Active Trading

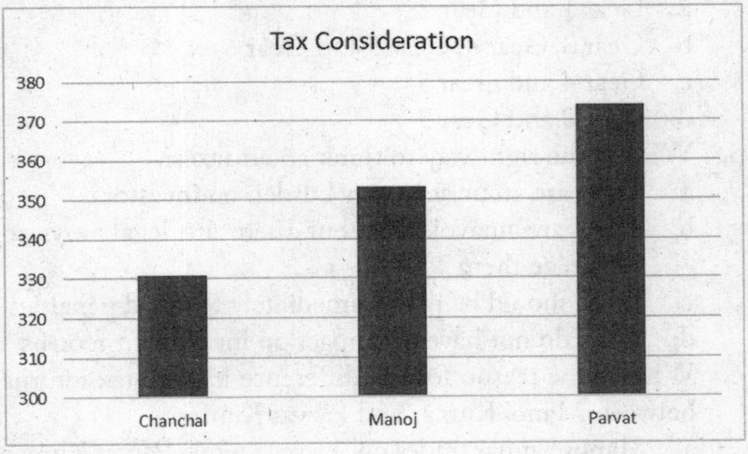

Check Your Understanding

1. How do most people view risk in the world of investment?
   a. As the risk of loss of principal
   b. As the possibility of high returns
   c. As uncertainty in the market
   d. As a combination of loss of principal and low returns

2. What are the factors that determine how much risk one can take?
   a. Market conditions and investment goals
   b. Mental makeup, attitude and safety margin
   c. Investment options and market conditions
   d. Personality and the stock market performance
3. What is the driving analogy used for in this chapter?
   a. To explain how different investments work
   b. To help readers understand their personality types
   c. To illustrate the relationship between risk and return
   d. To show how to use investment Gears to manage risk
4. According to Table 1.7, which investment Gears carry some risk of not meeting the goal of ₹10 lakh in the worst-case scenario?
   a. Gear 1 and Gear 2
   b. Gear 3, Gear 4, Gear 5 and Gear 6
   c. Gear 4 and Gear 5
   d. Gear 2 and Gear 3
5. What is the right way to think about taxes?
   a. Taxes are an unnecessary burden on investors
   b. Taxes are unavoidable, but there are legal ways to minimize them
   c. Taxes should be paid immediately to avoid penalties
   d. Taxes do not have an impact on investment returns
6. What is the reason for the difference in post-tax returns between Manoj Kumar and Parvat Kumar?
   a. Manoj Kumar trades once a year, while Parvat Kumar holds the same security for 10 years
   b. Parvat Kumar pays a lower tax rate than Manoj Kumar
   c. Parvat Kumar has a higher return on investment than Manoj Kumar
   d. Manoj Kumar pays a higher tax rate than Parvat Kumar.

Answers: 1–a, 2–b, 3–d, 4–b, 5–b, 6–a

Borrowing Money

Never spend your money before you have earned it.

—Thomas Jefferson

You must take risks, both with your own money or with borrowed money. Risk taking is essential to business growth.

—J. Paul Getty

There are a lot of different views on borrowing money and its wisdom in a financial plan. And they range from being the biggest mistake to being an essential ingredient.

The simplest question to ask about borrowing money is—for what purpose are you borrowing the money? Borrowing money to spend on your day-to-day living—like most credit card debt—is surely a recipe for poor financial health. Credit cards and general consumer debt are priced very expensively and would lead to poor financial outcomes.

There are, however, some specific cases in which borrowed money is a very important part of your financial plan. For example, borrowing money to buy a house for your family is a good use of borrowed money. A house is an asset which creates value over a long period of time. You can spread out the payment for the asset over the lifetime of the asset easily. This is quite a sensible thing to do.

Here is a simple way to look at it—don't borrow money to buy things that don't appreciate in value more than the interest rate you would pay on the borrowing. Or, at least, the decline in value less than the value they bring to you.

An example would be a car. It will depreciate in value, but if it provides comfort and efficiency in your commute, then it may be considered for purchase.

Another indicator is that if the repayment lasts longer than the benefit of what you buy with the borrowing, then don't borrow. For example, if you borrow to go on an expensive vacation, the benefit may last for a week or maybe even a few months in terms of a good feeling. But the payments will last a lot longer. You must compare the cost of getting the money—the interest cost—with the appreciation or benefit you receive from the use of the money.

Productive assets like a home or a stable investment (let's say a shop or office that can be given out for rent) can be purchased using borrowed money.

Tax Advantages of Borrowing

In many countries including India, interest paid on home loans is deductible for income tax purposes. This creates an advantageous situation for investors to borrow money even if they don't need it. While the tax rules are different for a self-occupied house and a rental house and beyond the scope of this book, the reduction in taxable income is often sufficient to make taking a loan to buy a house an attractive proposition. In Table 1.9, we show tax savings over 5 years.

TABLE 1.9 Impact of Tax Savings on Home Loan Interest

Summary	Amount (₹)
Property Value	1,00,00,000
Down Payment @20%	20,00,000
Loan Amount	80,00,000
Interest Rate	8.0%
Interest Paid in 5 years	30,48,503
Net Savings (20% tax rate)	6,09,701

Allocating Assets

Once you have determined your risk level and adjusted your investment strategy taking into account liquidity and tax considerations, you are ready to implement your plan. To implement any plan, you only need to select the right Gear as discussed in the section on 'Risk Tolerance'. You can select any Gear by simply mixing only two ingredients—debt investments and stocks (a diversified basket).

Debt

Debt refers to an investment in instruments where the duration of investment and return are fixed upfront, that is, they are 'fixed income' instruments. When you make a fixed deposit in a bank, the period of the investment and the rate of return are fixed at the time of investment. Bank fixed deposits are relatively safe investments. Banks are regulated by the RBI, which monitors the banks so that they are able to meet all their obligations. Deposits up to ₹5 lakh are insured by the Deposit Insurance and Credit Guarantee Corporation (DICGC). There have been at least 3 bank failures in India in the last 20 years. In each of these cases, the individual depositors were able to recover their investment, though they had to wait for some time for it.

There are also special mutual funds which are called 'money market funds' which invest in fixed return securities on behalf of their investors. Money market funds typically invest in a short duration, high quality debt. This allows investors to own many different debt securities through a single mutual fund.

The Government of India also issues investment instruments which have a fixed term and rate of return. For example, Bharat Bond is one such investment which is available to all investors. Many public and private sector companies issue similar debt instruments.

What is the difference between debt instruments issued by a bank, government, public sector company and private sector company? The biggest difference is 'credit risk'. Credit risk refers to the risk that the borrower may not be able to return the money they borrow. The banks and government are considered 'safe' as they have a low (but not zero) chance of not being able to pay back the money. But a riskier company (typically, an unregulated, small, private company) has a higher chance of a default. Therefore, the investment in fixed return products from riskier entities must have a higher rate of return to attract investors. Thus, the investor gets compensated for the higher amount of credit risk.

Online marketplaces can help you identify the best rates for debt products.

The other limitation in debt is the duration of the investment. Your money is locked up for a fixed term. This should be factored in while considering your investment profile. Longer lock up of money should give higher returns to compensate for this.

A list of funds which can give you debt returns is available on the website gulaq.com/MFmodelportfolio.

Indian Equity

The stock market is the primary source of growth of investment for investors. In the equity market, you purchase a small part of a business through 'shares'. Think of your neighbourhood store or a petrol pump. What if you could buy a business like that? The business will generate profits every year. Also, it will grow over time. Equity investment is the same thing, but instead of a small business that you own fully, in equity investment you buy a small part of a large business. If you buy shares of Reliance Industries, you become a part owner or shareholder of Reliance Industries—though, of course, a very tiny one. All its profits and future growth is owned by the shareholders of the company.

An equity investment generates returns through two methods—dividend and share price growth. Dividend is the amount of money that the business pays its shareholders every year—sometimes several times a year, sometimes nothing in a year. The share price growth is based on the growth in the prospects of the business over time. This is the crux of equity investment. Most businesses pay a limited amount of money as dividend—only 2–5% of the share price or even less. But the price of each share has the potential to grow as the business grows. Over time, this is significantly larger than the dividend that an investor receives.

In Table 1.10 you can see the two components of returns for the Nifty companies (the 50 largest companies). Of the total return over 10 years of 321%, 53% was generated from dividends and 268% was from the growth in the share price.

TABLE 1.10 Dividend and Capital Return

Stock Group	Nifty 50
Time Period	1 January 2013 to 31 December 2023
Total Return	321%
Dividend Return	53%
Stock Price Return	268%

Equity investments are made through brokerage accounts which help you buy and sell shares on stock markets like the NSE (National Stock Exchange) and BSE (Bombay Stock Exchange) in India. You can't buy shares in all the businesses that exist, only in the ones which are registered (or listed) on a stock exchange via a process called Initial Public Offer (IPO)—also known as 'going public'. Once the shares are listed, investors can buy and sell them in the stock market. This method allows any investor to own a small piece of any public company in the country. It is a truly amazing achievement of the capital market system that anyone can own a part of mega companies like Reliance or TCS with an investment of a few thousand rupees.

The stock markets constantly assess the prospects of every business. Every news item, every action of a competitor, every change in government regulations can make a difference in the prospects of an individual business. In addition, the market also factors in the impact of economic data like inflation, interest rates and cost of energy (electricity, petrol, diesel, etc.) on the business. This is the reason that, on a day-to-day basis, the prices gyrate all over the place as thousands of individuals assess the attractiveness of each business and their aggregate behaviour decides the share prices in the market.

Many people believe that the markets are rigged or controlled by a few people. These mysterious people or investors supposedly manipulate the prices in a way to create losses for individual investors. While this may be true for some fraudulent investors operating in companies with a very small public holding, in general this is not true for the overall market or even for most of the companies.

Other Assets

A good investment plan in India can be implemented with only two asset classes—debt and Indian equity. Many investors want to learn about other assets like gold and real estate, so I have included a brief description of each of them and my thoughts on how to include them into your investment plan.

NPS and PPF

The government allows only a few avenues to reduce taxes through investments. One of them involves accounts which contain savings for retirement or other long-term goals. These savings grow tax free in these accounts. Public Provident Fund (PPF) is a government scheme which provides fixed returns. As of 2023, the deposits in the scheme are also tax deductible up to ₹1.5 lakh under Section 80C. The interest income is also tax free. And even the withdrawal after maturity (currently 15 years, extendable in units of 5 years) is tax free.

The National Pension Scheme (NPS) is the newer retirement savings scheme by the government. The NPS scheme allows you to invest in the stock market through NPS-approved funds. Under this scheme, an additional investment amount of ₹50,000 is available for a total tax deduction of ₹2 lakh under section 80C.

Even though better investment products and returns may be available outside NPS, the tax benefits and the low expense ratio make them an attractive option to add to your portfolio. You must first max out investment in NPS (Table 1.11) before you consider other avenues.

This option is now slowly becoming unnecessary as under the provisions of Budget 2023, all such tax deductions are not

TABLE 1.11 NPS versus Mutual Fund

	NPS (₹)	**Mutual Fund (₹)**
Investible Money	2,00,000	2,00,000
Investible Money Post Tax (Assuming 20% Tax Rate)	2,00,000	1,60,000
Returns	10%	10%
Total Portfolio (Pre-Tax, after 30 Years)	3,61,88,685	2,89,50,948
Tax	–	48,30,190
Post-tax Portfolio	3,61,88,685	2,65,35,853

available under the new tax regime which offers the option of a lower income tax rate.

Foreign Equity

Indian companies are very visible and on top-of-the-mind of every investor, as many of them are often present in our everyday life. Through advertisements, daily consumption, news, TV programmes and discussions in social gatherings, we are constantly exposed to Indian businesses. But we should not forget that India has less than 5% of global businesses. The United States is still the world's largest market, with iconic companies like Apple, Microsoft, Google and Amazon.

Since diversification is a basic principle of sound investing, diversifying beyond India-specific risk is also important. There are several factors which would impact the growth of the stock market in India. Macroeconomic factors and the political situation in India can have an impact on the stock market returns for a long time. Investing in foreign markets diversifies that risk.

You may be worried that you don't know much about foreign markets, or even the process by which you can invest abroad. It is true that the process is still not as easy as investing within India. But there are several ways in which the diversification can be achieved without a lot of expertise or knowledge. There are mutual funds available in India which you can buy in your regular domestic account and get investment returns of foreign equity stocks. One of the funds that we use in our portfolios, based on our analysis up to December 2023, is Mirae Asset S&P 500 Top 50 ETF. A more updated list of funds appropriate for foreign investment is maintained on the website www.gulaq.com/modelportfolio.

If you wish to invest directly in foreign companies, even that is possible via the Liberalized Remittance Scheme (LRS). Under this scheme, every Indian can remit up to $250,000 every year towards investments abroad. But the tax treatment and the process make it cumbersome for regular investors, and they may need the help of professional consultants or financial managers.

Real Estate

Real estate is not a part of our model portfolio for three reasons. One is liquidity. The ability to convert a real estate investment into spendable cash is dependent on the market sentiment at that time. It can't be done in a hurry or with any certainty of the timeframes that will be involved. The value of stocks can go up or down, but you will able to convert them into cash quickly most of the time. Retail investors can usually convert their equity investments into cash any day the markets are open. Not so with an investment in real estate.

The second is lack of diversification. Because of the large amounts involved, most investors would not be able to invest in multiple real estate properties. This means you will have a big concentration risk—all or most of your money would be invested in a single property. What happens if the area in which you have the property becomes very crowded and unattractive due to congestion? Or a new highway passes close by bringing years of construction and noise, depressing the value of the property?

The third reason is the relative attractiveness of buying versus renting. In India, rents are 2–4% of the property value. On an average, the value of real estate appreciates at the rate of fixed deposits rather than the rate of growth in equity markets, as shown in Figure 1.6. This data is from 1937–2023. We have taken the data from the US market as a much longer data series is available there. We expect the trends to be similar in India. This means that the returns on investment in real estate will be lower than returns on investment in a diversified stock portfolio.

FIGURE 1.6 10-Year Annualized Rolling Returns of Equity (S&P) vs Real Estate and Other Assets

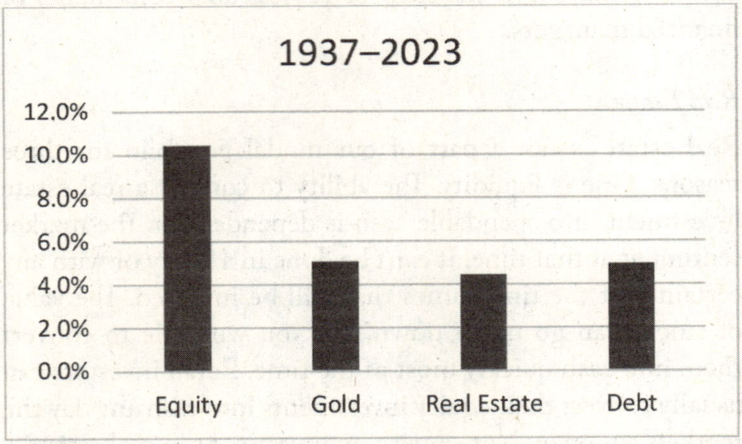

For these three reasons, we do not recommend real estate as a part of your savings portfolio.

However, home ownership is a goal for many people as a lifestyle choice and an emotional need. Many people prefer to live in a home they own. So you must save to fulfil your goal of home ownership. But do not invest in real estate as a part of your investment portfolio.

In the near future, we expect that real estate investments will become more attractive through the introduction and scaling up of investments called REIT (Real Estate Investment Trust). REITs are like mutual funds for real estate investments. A fund manager buys many real estate properties and you can buy a small share in this portfolio. This investment will address two of the problems—liquidity (you can sell your share of the portfolio to any other investor, just like mutual funds or stocks) and diversification—but not the third (growth in returns).

Gold

Gold is a favourite investment of many Indians. Indians are the largest buyers of gold in the whole world. In 2023, Indian consumers bought 747.5 metric tons of gold worth around ₹4,82,000 crore.

Gold is considered a traditional investment as it is a good store of value. For centuries, gold has kept its value, and most of the time, increased in value. But investment in gold has two shortcomings. One, it lacks underlying growth. Unlike equity investment in a business, gold is not a productive asset. A business grows over time and generates income. But if you buy a heavy necklace of gold and put it away in the safe deposit box, it will not generate a small gold ring over time. It does not become more productive over time. The second issue is that it does not have a predictable return pattern. While, on an average, investments in gold do earn returns similar to debt investments, they do not have the fixed return characteristics of debt investments. In a debt investment, the investment has a clear return expectation over a fixed period. Gold is not like that. Who can say whether gold will be more expensive or less in one year's time?

So gold is neither a productive asset which grows over time, like an equity investment, nor does it have a committed return, like a debt investment.

Many people consider gold as a hedge against inflation. Especially in the periods when inflation is high, they believe that gold will grow in value, thus providing protection. In Figure 1.7, we have shown the return on gold investment and inflation by the year. Every dark dot represents returns on gold and light dot represents the inflation rate. There are periods when gold did provide protection against inflation, like between 1970 and 1985. At the same time, from 1980 to 2005, it did not grow in value. A broad portfolio of stocks provides a much better protection against inflation.

The long-term returns on gold are similar to debt returns. So if you would like to keep some of your debt investment portfolio in gold, that is okay. But for the growth part of the portfolio, gold cannot compete with a diversified portfolio of equity investments.

Crypto

Crypto is the new kid on the block. Cryptos attract a lot of young people who are enamoured by the potential of very

FIGURE 1.7 Gold Return vs Inflation (US)

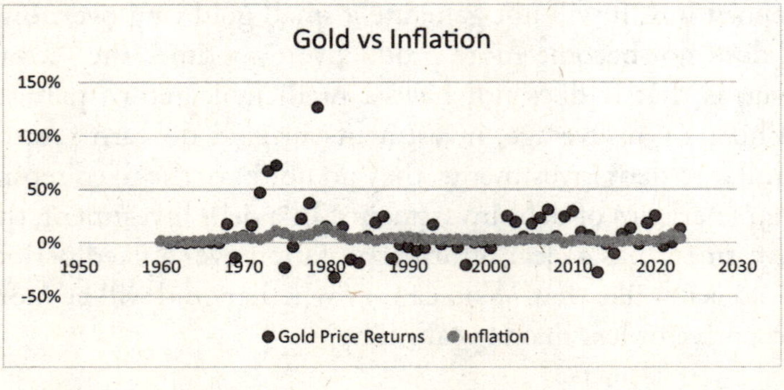

high profits in a short time. The underlying technology of crypto, called blockchain, has several advantages. It creates systems which allow people to exchange value without going through any trusted party (like a bank) in the middle. Today, if you want to pay someone, you either use a bank or an application like UPI. The bank or payment company are a trusted party in the middle, who enable you to transfer money in a reliable way. Cryptos can do the same thing, without using any trusted party in the middle. This is a revolutionary technology and concept.

The blockchain technology has many other applications which may be built in the near future. For example, Ethereum is a crypto currency which has capabilities to allow the development of applications on it. There are many faster and better competitors of Ethereum already.

So, it is difficult to say which crypto coin will produce large gains. There will be many fraudulent coins that will come up along the way. Several crypto currencies like Luna have crashed to a value of zero suddenly. There is a lot of uncertainty and risk in predicting the winners in the crypto arena. The regulators all over the world are looking at the impact of this new development. Many countries, including India, have severely restricted banks from dealing with cryptos. China has banned trading in cryptos altogether.

On top of the risks and unpredictability of cryptos and the regulations, there is the risk of underdeveloped, unregulated institutions. The exchanges and companies which provide access to crypto are not regulated by institutions like RBI or SEBI.

In 2005, Mt Gox was the largest exchange for crypto trading. It lost a lot of money due to security and fraud issues. In 2022, FTX was one of the largest exchanges in the world. It declared bankruptcy and caused a loss of probably billions of dollars to its investors.

So, for these reasons—difficulty in assessing the value, lack of regulation, potential for fraud—an average retail investor would do well to stay away from an investment in crypto. There will come a time in the future when the regulations around cryptos will be clear and there will be transparency in operations. That will be the opportunity to invest.

Insurance and Annuity

The main part of the investment journey is about allocating between equity and debt assets. So, what is the use of insurance and annuity products? Insurance products are designed to help overcome risks that individual investors can't overcome themselves. Take health insurance, for example. Every year, 2 people out of 10,000 will suffer a heart attack. The average cost of hospitalization for an open-heart surgery to clear the blockage is ₹5 lakh. Now, if 10,000 people bought an insurance cover of ₹1,000, then it can cover the cost of the treatment for the two people who suffer from the heart attack, without putting an extraordinary burden on the rest of 9,998 people. This is the fundamental benefit of insurance.

What are the risks that you need to cover through insurance? There are primarily three risks.

The first is health. As in the example, the cost of treatment is very high even though the chance that you will need the treatment is small. Unexpected healthcare cost is the largest reason pushing people into financial ruin.

The second risk is the early death of an earning member. Every family has some family member who is earning more than what they are spending on themselves. Thus, they support the rest of the family members or provide for the future needs of the family. In case of an untimely death of this member, the whole family will be short of money. So there is a need for life insurance to protect the dependent family members. In the event of an early death of the earning member, the insurance company will pay the family a lumpsum amount.

In India, insurance is still at a nascent stage. A majority of people are under-insured. In the normal course of things, the younger the person, the more life insurance they need to have. Think about it this way. The insurance amount should be equal to the current value of savings over their whole career. So, a 30-year-old, who is contributing ₹1 lakh every year towards family expenses and plans to work for 30 more years, should have a life insurance policy with a benefit of at least ₹30 lakh. A 60-year-old, who is about to retire, does not need to have a large life insurance policy as they do not have any savings potential left.

Finally, there is the third risk—the uncertainty of the duration of the retirement years. This is a tricky concept. Let's say you retire at the age of 65 and have enough savings to pay for a comfortable living till 80 years of age. That would appear to be reasonable as the average life expectancy of a 65-year-old is 80 years. But the average of 80 includes people who will live much lesser as well as much longer. In case you are one of the lucky ones who live to 90 years of age, then how will you pay your expenses from the age of 80 to 90? This is where annuity schemes come in.

An annuity product is a combination of insurance and investment. It protects against the uncertainty of how long you would need retirement savings. Let's say there are 10,000 people at the age of 65 who buy an annuity. On an average, they would live till the age of 80. If all of them have appropriate amounts of savings to fund retirement till 80, there will still be an imbalance. Some people, who die before the age of 80, will have excess savings. They would not require all their savings. The people who live beyond the age of 80 will be short of savings. The annuity product helps bridge the gap between the two groups. So everyone will receive the same amount of money every year till their death, no matter whether they live till 70, 80 or 90—or more. This is the benefit of annuity.

Of course, in every insurance product, there is a cost of buying the insurance. The company which manages the product has costs and needs to earn a profit on their effort. So an investor should shop carefully while buying the right product for their needs after comparing coverage and costs.

Check Your Understanding

1. Which of the following is true about implementing an investment plan?
   a. Risk tolerance is not a factor in implementing an investment plan
   b. Asset allocation is the most important outcome of an investment plan
   c. Liquidity and tax considerations are not important in implementing an investment plan
   d. Implementing an investment plan requires investing only in debt securities
2. What is the biggest difference between debt instruments issued by a government and a private sector company?
   a. Duration of investment and returns
   b. Credit risk
   c. Liquidity risk
   d. Market risk
3. Which of the following affect the price of shares in the stock market?
   a. Economic data like inflation and interest rates
   b. News about the company
   c. Actions of competitors
   d. All of the above

4. What is the difference between dividend return and stock price return in equity investment?
    a. Dividend return refers to the potential growth in the share price as the business grows, while stock price return is the amount of money that the business pays its shareholders every year
    b. Dividend return refers to the amount of money that the business pays its shareholders every year, while stock price return is the potential growth in the share price as the business grows
    c. Dividend return refers to the total return generated by an equity investment, while stock price return is the amount of money that the business pays its shareholders every year
    d. Dividend return and stock price return are the same thing
5. What is the benefit of investing in Public Provident Fund (PPF)?
    a. High returns on investment
    b. Easy withdrawal process
    c. Tax-deductible deposits and tax-free returns
    d. Guaranteed capital protection
6. What is the National Pension Scheme (NPS)?
    a. A retirement savings scheme by the Indian government
    b. A type of mutual fund for real estate investments
    c. A government scheme that provides fixed returns on investment
    d. An investment scheme that offers high tax benefits
7. Why is diversification beyond India-specific risk important for investors?
    a. To maximize returns on investment
    b. To invest in iconic companies like Apple and Amazon
    c. To minimize tax liabilities
    d. To reduce overall investment risk

8. What are some ways to invest in foreign equity markets for Indian investors?
    a. Via mutual funds and Liberalized Remittance Scheme
    b. Via commodity markets and foreign currency exchanges
    c. Via foreign banks and financial institutions
    d. Via real estate and debt markets
9. What is the reason behind the popularity of gold investment in India?
    a. High returns on investment
    b. Easy availability and low investment risk
    c. Cultural significance and perceived investment benefits
    d. Tax benefits and diversification opportunities
10. What is a potential solution for the liquidity and diversification problems associated with real estate investment?
    a. Foreign equity investment
    b. Public Provident Fund (PPF)
    c. National Pension Scheme (NPS)
    d. Real Estate Investment Trusts (REITs)

Answers: 1–b, 2–b, 3–d, 4–b, 5–c, 6–a, 7–d, 8–a, 9–c, 10–d

Investment Selection

NOW THAT YOU HAVE an asset allocation, you are ready to select some actual investments. The asset classes give you a broad outline of what your investment plan will look like. Within each investment class, you still have the task of selecting individual investments.

Active versus Passive Investment

First, a simple observation. The average person will achieve average return in the market. Let us take an example. Let us say there are 30 children in a class. The average marks obtained in the class will be the marks of an 'average' student. If everyone's parents expected their child to do better than average, it is not possible because, by definition, an average will have some people below and some people above the score. Similarly, in the investment world, the market return is the average of the returns of all the investors in the market. But some will earn more, some will earn less.

There are two types of investors—active investors and passive investors. The passive investors want to earn an average return. They assume that it is very hard—if not impossible—to outperform the market average. They know that if they invest in the market index, then they will achieve the average return of the market.

The active investors believe that they can do better than the average. But not everyone can be better than the average.

While it is possible that some investors outperform the index, it is impossible for a large majority of the investors to outperform the index.

So the investment choice—whether to be a passive investor or an active investor—depends on whether you or your advisor have the abilities to be better than an average investor. If you do, active investing will be beneficial. Till you develop such abilities, it is safer to be a passive investor and invest in the index.

Another factor in favour of passive investments is the lower cost of implementing a passive strategy. Investment managers who manage investments actively cost much more than those who manage passively. Even if you were to manage the investments yourself, there will be higher transaction costs as you chase the next best idea and trade actively. There will also be a higher effort required in implementing an active strategy.

John Bogle, the founder of Vanguard Group, says in *The Little Book of Common Sense Investing: The Only Way to Guarantee Your Fair Share of Stock Market Returns*, 'After the deduction of the costs of investing, beating the stock market is a loser's game.'

Side Bar: The Bet

Do you still believe that asking professionals to handle your investments can help you make better than average returns? So did Protege Partners, a fund-of-funds, whose job was to find and invest in good funds.

Warren Buffett, the legendary investment guru, famously bet Protege Partners in 2008 that investment in the index of 500 largest companies in the United States (called S&P 500) will outperform an investment in 5 funds selected by Protege Partners over the next 10 years. During the period of the bet, the group of hedge funds generated 22% against the 85.4% return of the index fund. The group of hedge funds only outperformed the index funds in 2 of the 10 years.

If by now you are convinced that nobody can outperform average returns, think again. Warren Buffett himself is an active investor. He has outperformed S&P 500 regularly since 1965. From 1965 to 2021, his investment company Berkshire Hathaway produced about 2 times the return of the S&P 500 index. So it is possible for at least a few professional investors to outperform the index. The question is how to find such investors.

Evaluating Active Managers

The first step in evaluating a product is to understand its benchmark. The products can have different characteristics. The fastest human runner will still be slower than the slowest car. We can't compare movement simply based on speed. Humans should be compared with average humans and cars with average cars. The mutual fund industry requires every fund to have a benchmark. For any investment, you must always ask the question—what is the benchmark for performance?

In the world of investment, the benchmark comes in the form of the risk profile of a fund. Some investment funds take a lot more risk than others like, say, a fund that is focused on small and emerging companies. If you compared this fund with the Nifty index, over time you would expect a higher return as it is taking more risk—which will show up in some years where it will underperform the Nifty in a big way. Still, the average performance over time should be higher than Nifty's.

There are also balanced funds which combine equity and debt investments. Such funds will perform less than the Nifty in the years when the index does well and do better in the years where the index loses money.

At Gulaq, we provide investment portfolios in six variants—the difference is in the mix of equity and debt investments. So the return and risk will also be different. To measure whether a product is doing well, we must compare it with a benchmark which combines the equity index (Nifty) with a debt index (say, fixed deposit rate) in the same proportion.

Second, you must understand the costs involved in investing. These include advisory fees, administration charges, brokerage fees and other fixed and variable fees. Obviously, the lower the fee, the better it is for the investor.

And finally, to complete the evaluation of an active manager, their performance should be measured over time. It is a truism in the investment world that only the funds and advisors who have had a good recent performance advertise their recent performance. But you must look at a long enough period to understand the real quality of performance. For equity funds that is 3–5 years.

For example, 2022 was a good year for large cap companies. Some funds which focus on large cap companies performed well compared to the benchmark (Nifty). About 62% of the funds outperformed the benchmark in a one-year period. However, only 19% outperformed the index in a 3-year or 5-year period.[6]

Building Your Own Portfolio

What if you wanted to build your own portfolio? How can you pick a good portfolio of stocks? There are many common sense approaches to do this. You should mainly look for companies which have the following:

1. Good products and market position, like Titan or Asian Paints
2. Strong profitability and operating margin

3. Positive momentum
4. Good return on equity, a good dividend payout ratio and so on

Any professional investor will list literally hundreds of factors to consider while trying to identify a good stock to invest in. This topic is covered in detail in 'Part 4: Taking It Further'.

Fees and Transaction Costs

Over time, fees and transaction costs eat up a large part of investment returns. An average large cap mutual fund has a total expense ratio (TER) of 2.15%. TER includes the base fee that the mutual fund company charges, its marketing fees and administrative and regulatory charges. If the average expectation of return in equity investment is 15%, then 2.15% represents more than 14% of this return.

You can also get exposure to large cap index funds with as little fees as 0.06%. Over a period of 10 years, that can make a difference of nearly 30% in your return.

There is a wide variation in the fees as well. In the same large cap mutual fund space, while the average TER is 2.15%, the charges of different funds range from 1.54% to 2.55%. SEBI placed a limit of 2.55% TER on 18 May 2023. Let us assume that two funds generated a return of 15% per annum. One fund has a TER of 1.54% and the other has a TER of 2.55%. Figure 1.8 shows the difference between the final amounts you will have after 20 years of investment in the two funds. The difference is almost 18% in the total sum.

If you trade in individual stocks yourselves, the brokerage rate can make a big difference to your net return. The brokerage charges can be as much as half of your profits of trading.

FIGURE 1.8 ₹100,000 Invested for 20 Years at 15% Per Annum Return

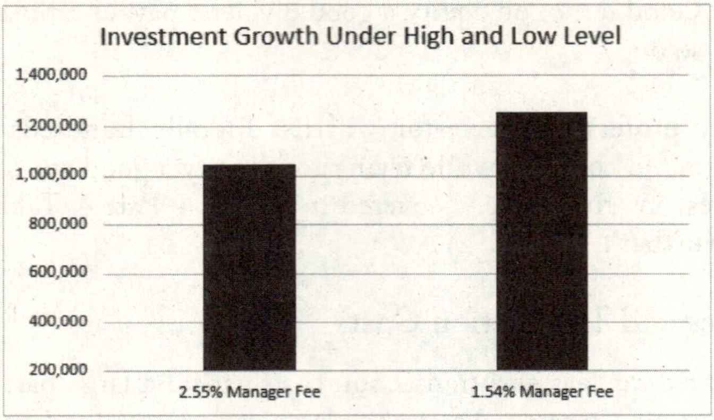

It is easy to check the total costs. Each mutual fund has to disclose its TER in their product documents as well as on their website. You must check the TER before making the investment. The returns of the investment are variable but costs are known upfront and always reduce your returns.

Even if you trade with a broker who offers zero brokerage fee, don't forget the transaction costs like Securities Transaction Tax (STT), Stamp Duty and other regulatory fees.

Check Your Understanding

1. What is the difference between an active investor and a passive investor?
   a. Active investors invest in the market index, while passive investors try to outperform the market average
   b. Active investors try to outperform the market average return, while passive investors want to get market return

   c. Active investors invest in the market index, while passive investors try to invest in individual stocks
   d. Active investors try to invest in ETFs, while passive investors invest in the mutual funds
2. What is the main factor in favour of passive investment compared with active investment?
   a. The ability to outperform the market average
   b. The lower cost compared to active investment
   c. The higher potential returns compared to active investment
   d. The ability to invest in individual stocks
3. Can anyone outperform the market index frequently?
   a. No, it is impossible for anyone to outperform the market index
   b. Yes, it is possible for everyone to outperform the market index
   c. Yes, it is possible for a few investors to outperform the market index
   d. None of the above
4. When evaluating an investment product, what is the first step you should take?
   a. Understanding its benchmark
   b. Measuring its performance over time
   c. Analysing its costs
   d. Checking its risk profile
5. How much of an average large cap mutual fund's returns can be eaten up by fees over 10 years?
   a. 2%
   b. 10%
   c. 13%
   d. 30%
6. What are some transaction costs to consider when trading single stocks?
   a. Brokerage rate

b. Securities Transaction Tax
c. Stamp Duty
d. All of the above

Answers: 1–b, 2–b, 3–c, 4–a, 5–d, 6–d

Mechanics of Investment

CONGRATULATIONS, YOU HAVE ALMOST completed this section on how to develop a simple investment plan which will outperform more than half of all the lay investors who try to pick stocks or time the markets. In this section we will review the actual mechanics of how to invest. We will introduce the different types of market intermediaries, accounts and other operational aspects of actually investing in the markets. If you have been trading or investing in stock markets for some time, then you can safely skip this section. If you are confused about any particular aspect of market structure, then you can read only that section selectively.

Investments can be made through the following instruments:

- Mutual Funds
- ETFs
- Stocks
- Fixed Deposits

There are many other instruments like futures, options, bonds, corporate bonds, private funds and so on, but they are outside the scope of this book.

Mutual Funds

A mutual fund is a type of investment that collects money from many investors and invests it in a variety of securities, such as stocks, bonds and money market instruments. Mutual funds are managed by professional investment managers who are responsible for selecting the securities that the fund invests in and for making decisions about when to buy and sell those securities. Mutual funds are regulated and monitored by market regulators—like SEBI (Securities and Exchange Board of India) in India.

Mutual funds offer a number of advantages to investors:

- Diversification: By investing in a mutual fund, you can get instant diversification, which means that your money is spread out across a variety of securities. This helps to reduce your risk because if one security performs poorly, the gains in other securities in the fund may help to offset the losses.
- Systematic Investment Plans and Small Investments: Mutual funds allow investors to invest small amounts of money. Most funds have a minimum investment amount of only ₹500. Mutual funds also allow you to set up a periodic investment plan. For such systematic investment plans (SIP), the minimum investment amount may even be lower at ₹100 or ₹200.
- Professional Management: Mutual funds are managed by professional investment managers who have the expertise and resources to research and select securities. This can save you time and money, as you do not have to do all the research yourself.
- Liquidity: Mutual funds are highly liquid, which means that you can easily buy and sell units in the fund. This makes them a good option for investors who need to be able to access their money quickly.
- Tax Efficiency: Mutual funds are tax efficient, as all the buying and selling within the fund does not have a tax impact on the investor. The investor only pays tax when they sell the mutual fund units.

When you invest in a mutual fund, you are essentially buying a share of the fund's portfolio. The value of your investment will go up or down with the value of the securities in the fund's portfolio. Mutual funds typically charge fees, such as management fees and other expenses (TER), which are deducted from the fund's gross value before declaring its net asset value (NAV).

There are nearly 50 mutual fund companies in India. Almost all large banks and financial institutions have a separate mutual fund company.

All mutual funds have two kinds of plans:

Regular Plan: These mutual fund plans are sold by a distributor like your local bank or a brokerage house. The distributor is paid a commission by the mutual fund company for their efforts. While the distributor does not charge anything to the investor, the investor's overall cost of investing in the mutual fund includes the distributor's commission.

Direct Plan: Every mutual fund, by SEBI regulation, is also available directly from the mutual fund company. In this case, there are no distribution costs. Typically, the Direct Plan version of a fund is 0.5–1% cheaper (i.e., the return to the investor is higher by 0.5–1%) than the Regular Plan of the same fund. Remember, you receive this extra amount every year and not just at the time of purchase, so the earnings can be substantial over the years.

ETFs

ETFs, or Exchange Traded Funds, are very similar to mutual funds, with one major difference—an ETF is bought or sold on a stock exchange like a stock. The price of an ETF is the price at which it is available on the stock exchange and it changes during the trading hours when the stock markets are open. This is different from a mutual fund, which is priced only once a day—at the end of the day, based on the actual price of the investments that the fund holds.

Stocks

You can also buy securities in specific companies—that is, their stocks or shares—which are listed on a stock exchange. Initially, these companies sell their shares to the general public through an Initial Public Offer (IPO). Then these shares are made available to be bought and sold on the stock exchange.

Fixed Deposits

Fixed deposits are offered by banks or non-banking financial companies (NBFCs). There are many websites which offer to search the best rate of a fixed deposit for you. You can do so using Stable Money, Bank Bazaar and Paisa Bazaar, among other sites. Fixed deposits are considered relatively safe investments as RBI regulates and monitors banks. This does not mean that a bank can't default on its obligations, and in an extreme case, depositors can lose money. DICGC only provides insurance for amounts up to ₹5 lakh per individual.

To implement your investment plan you would need to open several accounts. It is important that you understand the relationship between these accounts.

Brokerage Account

You open a brokerage and trading account with a stockbroker. There are nearly a thousand stockbrokers in India. All stockbrokers are regulated by SEBI. When you open an account with a stockbroker, you can access the stock exchanges. You can see the price at which a stock is available in the stock market at any time. The trading account is only for transacting in stocks, it does not hold your securities.

There are two distinct types of brokers:

- Full Service Brokers: Typically a part of a large bank like HDFC, Kotak or ICICI, full service brokers provide a quick facility to the customers to open a brokerage account and invest in the stock market. The fees reflects a full service model. They provide research and recommendations along with access to the stock market.
- Discount Brokers: About 10 years ago, a new breed of mostly online brokers sprang up. These brokers, like Zerodha, Groww, 5paisa and others, allow online access to trading. They typically offer very low or even no brokerage charges for trading in stocks. They provide the convenience and low costs of an online business. They are convenient for people doing buy–sell transactions frequently.

Depository Account

Your securities are held in a Depository Account (called a 'Demat Account'). Depository accounts are held at one of the two depositories in India—NSDL and CDSL. You receive communication from these depositories about your security holdings. You can also check your holdings by accessing your depository account directly with the depository. However, to open and operate the account, you need the services of a Depository Participant (DP). There are about 300 depository participants (DPs) who work with brokers. The larger brokerage houses have their own DPs. The smaller brokers use depository services of other firms.

Check Your Understanding

1. Which of the following is not an investment instrument?
    a. Mutual funds
    b. ETFs
    c. Trading account
    d. Stocks
    e. Bonds
2. Which of the following is not an advantage of investing in mutual funds?
    a. Diversification
    b. Professional management
    c. Liquidity
    d. Tax efficiency
    e. High minimum investment amount
3. Which of the following is the difference between a mutual fund and an ETF?
    a. A mutual fund is priced only once a day, while an ETF is priced continuously throughout the trading session
    b. A mutual fund is bought and sold through an exchange, while an ETF is bought and sold through a distributor
    c. A mutual fund is managed by a professional investment manager, while an ETF is not
    d. A mutual fund is considered to be a safer investment than an ETF
    e. A mutual fund is subject to more taxes than an ETF
4. The stocks you buy are held at what institution?
    a. Broker
    b. Depository Participant (DP)
    c. Depository
    d. Exchange

Answers: 1–c, 2–e, 3–a, 4–c

A Simple 10-Point Checklist for Investors

In Part 1 of this book, I have laid out a simple method that will help investors generate better than average returns for building their savings and investment plan. I will summarize this as a simple checklist.

1. Have the right expectations. From historical data, your long-term return from investing in stock markets will be about 15%. This is significantly better than debt returns which will average about half of this.
2. Evaluate your risk tolerance. Based on your age, earning levels, savings and goals, you should set your risk tolerance. Your emotional ability to handle swings in the market is also important.
3. Select the right asset allocation for your risk level. The right mixture of debt and equity is needed for your level of risk tolerance. This is for the overall portfolio, not for each investment. You may hold a small amount of risky investments in an overall conservative portfolio or vice versa.
4. Select the right investments from debt and equities to implement your asset allocation. The right securities should perform as well as the benchmark for that security. Start with index funds. Only when you have significant knowledge and experience of investments, should you move to investing beyond index funds. Pick a more complicated product only if you are confident about the ability of your investment manager to do better than the index.
5. Pay attention to the transaction costs and total expenses related to each investment. Also know about the tax treatment of the investment product. But don't focus only on costs, expenses and taxes—compare post-expense, post-tax returns.

6. Monitor the performance periodically. But not daily. A good frequency is quarterly or even annually.
7. Rebalance your portfolio to the desired asset allocation at least once a year.
8. Don't pay much attention to thematic investment advice—momentum, value, sector specific, small-cap funds and so on. Stay with equity and debt investments. Also, don't pay attention to specific stock tips. It is a game heavily stacked against you.
9. Besides the home you live in and the jewellery you enjoy using, don't use real estate and gold as a part of your regular savings portfolio.
10. Protect against specific risks—healthcare risk through health insurance, death of an earning member through life insurance and the risk of longer than expected retirement period through annuities.

Part 2

Avoiding the Noise

In God we trust; all others must bring data.

—W.E. Deming

IF YOU HAVE READ so far, you might be thinking, investing is simple. I have it all figured out now. It is true—concepts of disciplined investing are very simple. The problem comes in the implementation discipline. We are constantly distracted or led astray by tremendous internal and external noise.

Internal noise is the emotional swings that impact all of us. This is a big hurdle in generating returns on our investment. We will cover several examples of emotional intelligence that we need to develop to be a good investor.

Then there is the external noise. We are constantly bombarded by ideas on how to generate high returns. An important part of learning is to unlearn what does not work. The goal is to move from anecdotes of phenomenal profits to a systematic, repeatable method. We will examine hard evidence to see if some of the popular myths provide any advantage in investing. A broken watch is right twice a day. So just because at some point some view resulted in a profit does not mean that overall it is good advice. We need to evaluate each claim exhaustively over a long period of time and determine its effectiveness.

Sure-Shot Tip

In all of investing, the most dangerous words are, 'This is a sure-shot investment.' Usually exchanged between friends in hushed tones after imbibing some alcoholic beverage or on a golf course. The information is shared as a testament to the friendship that the two persons have and is meant to indicate loyalty and desire to benefit the other person.

This type of advice is similar to the idea of getting a tattoo after a night out. At that moment it sounds exciting, brave and even the most logical thing to do. But in the light of logic and rational thought later, it is never the sensible thing to do.

The most important noise to avoid in investing are such tips. The tips sometimes may even come from very impressive-looking experts on credible TV shows.

Emotional Roller-Coaster

We have met the enemy and he is us.

—Walt Kelly

OUR OWN EMOTIONS ARE the most difficult adversaries to conquer for building a disciplined investment approach. Greed, fear, biases—all play a role in distorting our ability to invest properly.

Morgan Housel's bestselling book *The Psychology of Money: Timeless Lessons on Wealth, Greed, and Happiness* covers many emotional and psychological factors that impact our relationship with money. I will discuss some of the main ones here.

Greed and fear lead people to believe in market timing. Enormous effort is spent in trying to figure out when to start investing or to reduce the investments in the stock market. As we will see in the section 'Market Timing', this is an impossible task. Markets are very efficient in factoring all the information into the stock price very quickly. Many experts have developed extremely fast and sophisticated computer systems to react to all kinds of information in a few milliseconds. So a retail investor who is trying to process historical information and decide what to do based on that—whether to invest or redeem—is reacting to stale information which has already been factored into the stock price.

Then there are biases that affect all humans. Investors think of themselves as rational persons, who make all decisions based on available data, like a precise calculator. In reality, we behave like drunk gamblers, betting on a gambling table in a casino. Some of the now famous biases were discovered by eminent scientists, Daniel Kahneman and Amos Tversky. In experiment after experiment, they demonstrated that all people—ranging from the uneducated to the well-educated and sophisticated—regularly make large mistakes due to their inherent biases. This branch of study is called behavioural economics and it took several decades for people to accept it as legitimate. While Daniel Kahneman did most of the work with his partner, Amos Tversky, in the 1970s, he received the Nobel Prize only in 2002 and probably became widely known only a decade later.

Availability

We overemphasize things which we can easily recollect because they are readily available in our memory. In the investment world, an interesting example of this happened in 2012. Do you remember the sensational hit song from that year—'Gangnam Style'? The global popularity of this song led to an 800% increase in the stock price of DI Corp, a South Korean semiconductor-testing equipment maker.[7] The only link between the two was that the DI Corp was led by the father of the singer Psy!

More recently, GameStop became a famous meme stock primarily driven by internet chat group participants taking on sophisticated hedge funds who had written off the company. A big part of the motivation for investors was the familiarity with the company which sells video games from stores in the shopping malls around the United States.

This is partially the reason that Facebook, Amazon, Apple, Netflix and Google (FAANG) became hugely popular stocks and grew rapidly in value.

On the other hand, in India, stocks like SRF, which has returned almost 50% a year from 2012 to 2022, is not very well known as it does not have many retail products.

Loss Aversion

Simply put, the pain of losing ₹100 is more than the joy of gaining ₹200. Kahneman conducted many experiments to measure loss aversion accurately. In one experiment, he offered to flip a coin. If the person lost the toss, he would lose $10. He then asked several people what they would need to win for them to accept the bet. The answer averaged $20. So he concluded that, on an average, we are twice as averse to losing than winning.

This loss aversion plays a role in investing. Once a person invests, if the stock goes below the price paid, it is very difficult for the person to sell it and concretize the loss. Till the time they sell, the loss is notional. It only becomes real once the stock is sold. As a result, people keep holding on to their losing investments for much longer than they logically should.

> Chanchal Kumar and Parvat Kumar are two brothers with a similar personality. Both of them discuss buying stock of company A which is at ₹100 per share. Chanchal is quick to implement and buys 100 shares at ₹100 each. Parvat is a little slow and forgets to buy. After a few days they realize that the stock is now at ₹90. Parvat is not sure that the stocks in Company A is a great investment, so he decides not to buy. Chanchal agrees with his brother but he does not want to sell as he has lost some money and wants to make it up. He promises himself that he will sell the share as soon as the price recovers to his purchase price, ₹100.

Many readers would not find this scenario odd at all. But it is! Just because Chanchal owns the stock, he finds it worth holding. And Parvat does not find it worth investing, as he does not hold it.

Hindsight Bias

Human beings have an amazing ability to find reason for everything that happens. If your favourite team loses a match or an unlikely candidate wins an election, you will be ready with an explanation. It is the same with stock market investments. If the market falls 10%, everyone feels that it was obvious that the market was due for a correction.

This leads to a belief that if it is obvious to us now, then the next time we can be a little more attentive and know about the event in advance. The reality is that predicting the direction of the market in the short term is just not possible. Don't let people make you feel bad during the lean periods that you are foolish to be invested in the stock market—you should have known better and sold off in time. There will always be periods where the markets will gain a lot and the same friends would be wringing their hands on the sidelines. Stay invested and committed to your investment plan.

Check Your Understanding

1. What is the main challenge in implementing disciplined investing?
   a. The complexity of investment concepts
   b. The lack of external noise in the market
   c. The emotional swings that impact investors
   d. The absence of anecdotes of phenomenal profits

2. What is the impact of biases in investing?
    a. They help investors make rational decisions based on data
    b. They distort an investor's ability to invest properly
    c. They ensure that all investors behave like precision calculators
    d. They help investors develop a systematic, repeatable method
3. What is the 'Availability' bias?
    a. Overemphasizing things which are readily available in memory
    b. Thinking of yourself as a rational person
    c. The pain of losing being more than the joy of gaining
    d. Developing fast and sophisticated computer systems
4. What is the impact of loss aversion on investing?
    a. It makes it easier for investors to sell their losing investments
    b. It leads investors to hold their losing investments for much longer than they should
    c. It makes investors more willing to take risks
    d. It ensures that all investments generate high returns

Answers: 1–c, 2–b, 3–a, 4–b

Golden Cross

THE NEWSPAPERS, POPULAR FINANCIAL websites, even TikTok is filled with stock market advice. In a major financial newspaper, a headline read, 'Golden Cross, Ahoy! Sensex, Nifty Charts Drop Hints This Rally Has Legs'. Golden Cross refers to an event when a short-term indicator, like a 30-day simple moving average (SMA), crosses a long-term trend, like a 120-day SMA. There are other headlines which have 'Head and Shoulders', 'Double Bottoms', 'Bullish Flag' and dozens of other imaginatively named patterns. The proponents of these chart indicators say that emotions drive markets and the price charts reveal the emotions of the markets. Reading these patterns, these people say they can decipher the moves the market will make next. This method of predicting price movement based on review of historical price and volume information is called 'technical analysis'.

This is an idea which has been around for at least a couple of centuries. No less an authority than Charles Dow, who co-founded the *Wall Street Journal*, published hundreds of editorials on technical analysis.

Stepping even further back, predicting the future by recognizing a pattern is a fundamental human cognitive capability. As humans evolved, their ability to recognize patterns and react with appropriate response increased and so did their chances of survival. We needed to distinguish whether that silhouette in the distance was a lion or a deer. We needed to know if the wind and temperature pattern indicated an impending storm so all of us could seek shelter.

This need to predict the future exists even now. When we see a chart, it is our deep innate desire to see a pattern which can help us decide better. If we see a pattern of crossover, which is sometimes followed by a price increase, we want to believe that we have the ability to predict the future price increase. In *How to Create a Mind*, Ray Kurzweil presented a theory that human neocortex evolved to recognize patterns. This part of the brain is specifically present in mammals and constitutes 80% of the weight of the brain.

The important question is, does this type of pattern recognition work in helping to predict stock price movement?

Let us examine one of the most common of these patterns—the Golden Cross, where the 30-day SMA crosses the 120-day SMA. Let us evaluate it for Britannia shares. Figure 2.1 shows an example of how a Golden Cross trade works. On 21 July 2016, Britannia's 30-day SMA crossed the 120-day SMA. This is supposed to mean that we should buy the stock. Then on 15 November 2017, the 30-day SMA went below the 120-day SMA. This is supposed to indicate that we should sell the stock. In this case, the trade produced a profit of 4.07%, in line with the hypothesis about Golden Cross.

FIGURE 2.1 Simple Moving Average

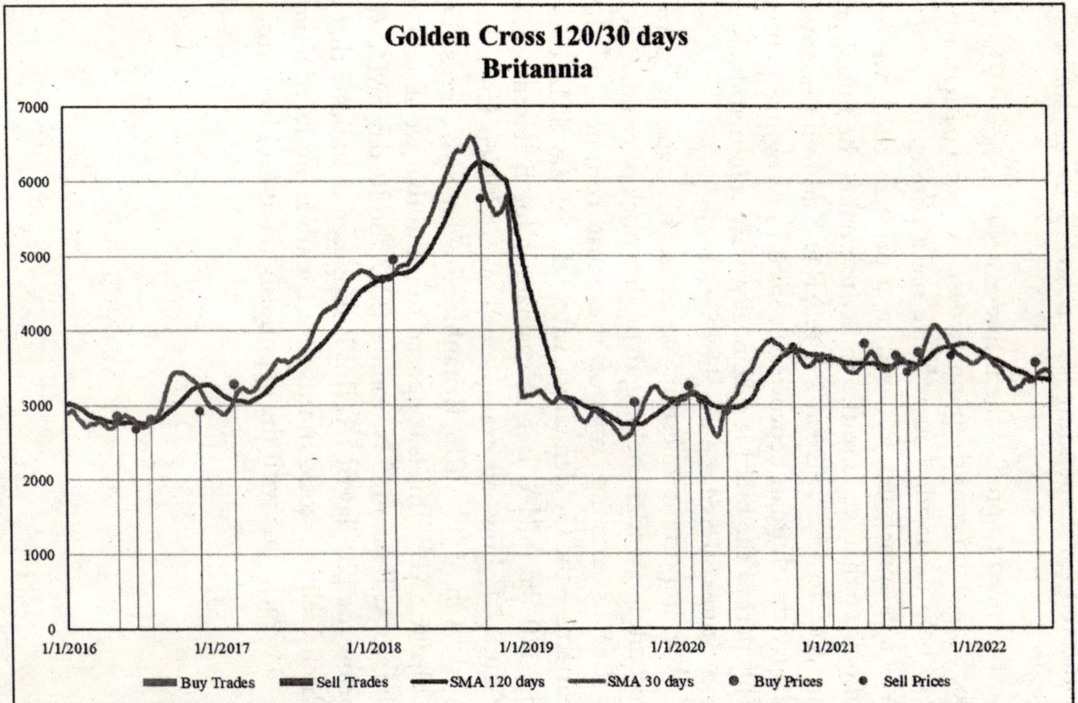

But what would happen over a longer period? Between 2016 and 2022 (Table 2.1 and 2.2), Britannia exhibited the Golden Cross 12 times. The average position lasted 3.8 days before reversing. In Table 2.1, we can see that the 8 trades produced a very good return of 73.4%. It is not quite as high as the Nifty Index returns over the same period, but it is still good. However, from 2021 to 2022, the 4 trades produced a negative return of -13.4%. So when examined over the whole period, the Golden Cross hypothesis does not pan out.

TABLE 2.1 Britannia Golden Cross Performance 2016–2020

Period of Evaluation	**1 Jan 2016–31 Dec 2020**
Number of completed trades	8
Profitable trades	4
Unprofitable trades	4
Total profit over the period	73.4%
Nifty return over the period	84.8%

TABLE 2.2 Britannia Golden Cross Performance 2021–2022

Period of Evaluation	**1 Jan 2021–30 Jun 2022**
Number of completed trades	4
Profitable trades	1
Unprofitable trades	3
Total profit over the period	–13.4%
Nifty return over the period	24.1%

Now let us examine this hypothesis across all the securities in Nifty 50 during the same period. In this analysis, we took the data of 50 securities over 6 years. Every time the market exhibited a Golden Cross, we bought the stock. And sold it when the reverse happened. The results are shown in Table 2.3.

TABLE 2.3 Nifty 50 Securities Golden Cross Trades

Period of Evaluation	**1 Jan 2016–30 Jun 2022**
Number of completed trades	514
Profitable trades	205
Unprofitable trades	309
Total profit over period	35%
Nifty return over the period	108%

In the next few pages, we will evaluate the results of trading using some of the popular technical indicators.

One momentum indicator is called Relative Strength Indicator (RSI). It was developed by J. Welles Wilder Jr and described in his book *New Concepts in Technical Trading Systems*, first published in 1978. RSI is a momentum indicator which uses average profit during periods with price increase and decrease in the recent past to determine whether the stock is overbought (indicating a potential price decrease) or oversold (indicating a potential price increase). Table 2.4 and Figure 2.2 present the results of trading using this indicator with a traditional cut-off of 30% for a buy signal and 70% for a sell signal.

TABLE 2.4 Nifty 50 Securities RSI Trades

Period of Evaluation	**1 Jan 2016–30 Jun 2022**
Number of completed trades	45
Profitable trades	25
Unprofitable trades	20
Total profit over period	–22.5%
Nifty return over the period	108%

FIGURE 2.2 Relative Strength Indicator (RSI)

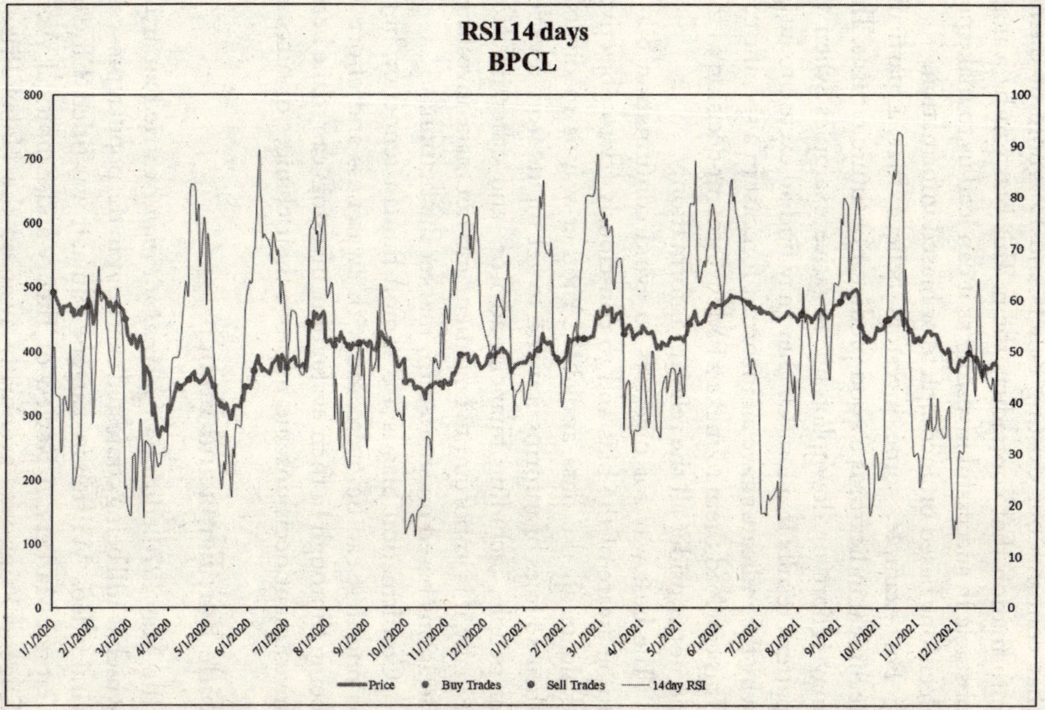

Side Bar: Confirmation Bias

Confirmation bias is the tendency to seek information that confirms our existing beliefs and to ignore or dismiss information that contradicts them. This bias can be a major obstacle in successful investing as it can lead us to make poor decisions based on incomplete or biased information.

For example, some investors believe that a particular technical indicator is a good predictor of future returns. They may ignore or downplay any negative examples when the pattern results in a loss. Or they may find an excuse to justify why the indicator gave an incorrect forecast in a specific case. This can lead them to make a bad investment decision as they do not consider all the relevant information.

The best way for investors to avoid confirmation bias is to be aware of the bias and to consciously try to objectively evaluate all the data available. Another way is to diversify their sources of information and to get inputs from a variety of people, including financial advisors and other investors. Finally, it is important to be patient and not make investment decisions based on short-term market fluctuations.

Confirmation bias is a common human tendency, but it is one that can be overcome with awareness and effort. By being thorough in their evaluation, investors can make better investment decisions and improve their chances of success.

Side Bar: Fama and French

The May 1970 edition of *Journal of Finance* carried an article which is still being contested every day in the popular press and viral videos. Written by Eugene Fama, it was titled 'Efficient Capital Markets: A Review of Theory and Empirical Work'. Eugene Fama was eventually awarded the Nobel Prize in 2013. The question he and his team were trying to answer was whether it was possible to 'beat the market'. He defined an 'efficient' market as one in which security prices 'fully reflected' all the available information. Can there be some information available today, which could tell us about the returns that we can achieve tomorrow? His conclusion was, 'No, it is not possible.'

The simplest form, also called the 'Weak Form of Efficient Market', says that there is nothing in the price data itself that can reliably predict future returns. This would mean all kinds of technical indicators and chart indicators are worthless and incapable of predicting future returns.

The other extreme is the 'Strong Form of Efficient Market'. In this type of a market, no information, whether known by all the investors or only by a privileged few, can predict future price movements. The belief here is that as soon as some people have the information, they would act on it and it would immediately get reflected in the price of the security.

This form of an Efficient Market only exists in theory books. As endless cases of insider trading around the world prove, extraordinary returns can be generated by using insider or privileged information.

In the middle of the two extremes of Weak and Strong Form of Efficient Markets lies the Semi-Strong Form of Efficient Markets. In this, the hypothesis is that the use of any kind of publicly known information—but excluding information known only to insiders—cannot produce incremental returns.

The 1992 paper of Fama and French[8] estimated returns using a three-factor model that identified three relevant factors using which one could generate returns better than the index. Subsequently, they expanded the list to five (and in some cases to six) factors.

Since then, researchers have identified many more factors by combining multiple pieces of information which help to generate extra returns. By recent count,[9] over 300 such factors have been identified.

Fama and French went on to partner with David Booth to set up an investment management firm, Dimensional Funds, which seeks to perform better than the market index using multifactor models.

Conclusion

The conclusion from all these rigorous tests is that using a technical indicator which relies on the price and volume information alone does not produce good returns. So stop wasting your time looking at simple charts, indicators, oscillators and so on.

Check Your Understanding

1. Why do humans have a deep innate desire to see patterns?
   a. To make better decisions
   b. To increase their chances of survival
   c. To predict the future
   d. All of the above
2. What is the Relative Strength Indicator?
   a. An indicator that uses moving averages to determine, buy and sell signals
   b. An indicator that measures the momentum of a stock
   c. An indicator that identifies patterns in stock charts
   d. An indicator that predicts the future price of a stock
3. What is confirmation bias?
   a. When the investor waits for confirmation before investing
   b. When the investor only uses information which confirms their existing views
   c. When investor trades only on information confirmed from multiple sources

4. What is Efficient Market Theory?
    a. Only efficient traders can make money in stock markets
    b. Markets are efficient in producing profits for traders who use technical analysis carefully
    c. Markets are efficient in reflecting all information in the stock price

Answers: 1–c, 2–b, 3–b, 4–c

Flavour of the Month

We often hear about theme-based investment plans. With names like 'Green Energy' or 'The Great Indian Middle Class', they make a convincing argument which appeals to our common sense. We know that the era of oil is coming to an end and alternate sources of energy will grow rapidly as they are being supported by governments around the world. It makes sense to invest in companies focused on green energy. We also know that India is a fast-growing economy and companies focused on serving the needs of the rapidly growing middle class will do well.

The challenges with such thematic investments are two. One is the effort and knowledge required to analyse the innumerable themes available in the market. In each theme, there is a perfectly rational, populist logic which justifies why the theme will perform well. The effort required to understand and select a viable theme is significant. It is less challenging than trying to understand the performance of a single company but still pretty daunting for a person with a full-time job and limited resources to do the research.

The second challenge with thematic investing is that the theme invariably goes through cycles. While the broad theme remains valid for years, in between the prices of individual stocks vary so much that they can overwhelm the returns of the theme—again, posing the challenge of adjusting your view.

Sector Investing

Take, for example, the theme of the growing middle class in India. The performance of the consumer discretionary companies over the period 2008–2023 is shown in Figure 2.3.

FIGURE 2.3 Performance of Consumer Discretionary Companies vs Nifty

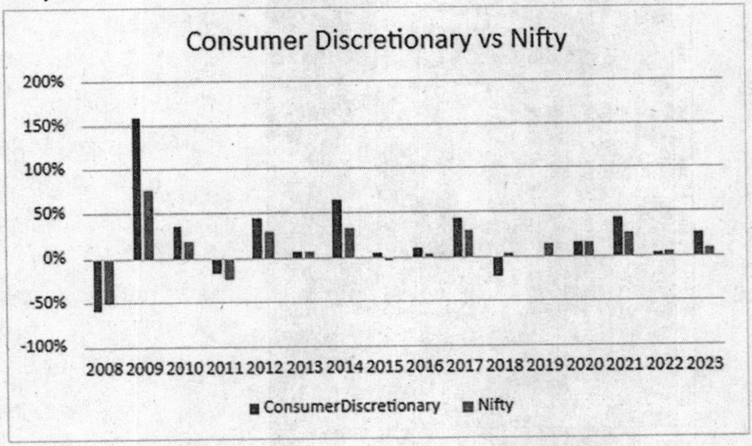

In Figure 2.4, we have presented the results of the major sectors/themes over 16 years, from 2008 to 2023. Each of the sectors out-performed the overall index in some of the years. However, over the whole period, none of the sectors could perform better than the overall index, especially when we adjust the data for risk.

FIGURE 2.4 Sector Performance

Utilities	UTIL
Industrials	IND
Real Estate	RE
IT	IT
Materials	MAT
Consumer Discretionary	CD
Communications	COMM
Energy	EN
Financials	FIN
Consumer Staples	CS
Healthcare	HC

2008	2009	2010	2011	2012	2013	2014	2015	2016	2017	2018	2019	2020	2021	2022	2023
CS -20%	MAT 120%	HC 33%	CS 5%	FIN 46%	IT 53%	IND 55%	HC 19%	MAT 30%	RE 78%	IT 24%	RE 29%	HC 52%	UTIL 67%	UTIL 43%	RE 27%
HC -32%	IT 112%	CD 31%	HC -12%	RE 44%	HC 20%	CD 52%	CS 8%	EN 21%	MAT 41%	CS 17%	EN 19%	IT 46%	IND 52%	IND 21%	CD 23%
UTIL -46%	CD 105%	FIN 30%	IT -13%	CS 41%	COMM 15%	HC 44%	COMM 5%	UTIL 15%	COMM 40%	FIN 3%	FIN 16%	UTIL 38%	RE 52%	FIN 14%	IND 21%
FIN -61%	IND 87%	CS 29%	COMM -16%	CD 39%	CS 12%	FIN 40%	IT 5%	FIN 13%	IND 40%	EN 0%	IT 12%	MAT 35%	IT 45%	CS 12%	HC 20%
EN -62%	RE 81%	IT 28%	CD -17%	HC 35%	CD 7%	MAT 32%	CD 4%	CD 11%	FIN 37%	HC -4%	COMM 9%	IND 23%	MAT 44%	EN 12%	CS 10%
COMM -62%	FIN 78%	COMM 9%	EN -24%	IND 26%	EN 2%	UTIL 24%	EN 1%	CS 4%	CS 35%	IND -10%	UTIL 5%	CD 22%	CD 36%	MAT 6%	MAT 9%
IT -70%	EN 63%	EN 8%	UTIL -32%	MAT 25%	FIN -6%	CS 24%	IND 1%	RE 2%	CD 34%	UTIL -10%	MAT 4%	COMM 20%	COMM 31%	CD 3%	IT 9%
CD -80%	HC 58%	MAT 4%	FIN -36%	EN 17%	MAT -6%	EN 24%	UTIL 0%	IND 2%	EN 30%	MAT -12%	CS 3%	RE 20%	EN 25%	COMM -1%	FIN 9%
IND -81%	UTIL 48%	IND 0%	MAT -37%	UTIL 13%	UTIL -11%	IT 20%	MAT -8%	IT -4%	UTIL 29%	CD -22%	HC 1%	EN 19%	FIN 19%	RE -6%	EN 9%
MAT -92%	CS 44%	UTIL -5%	RE -50%	COMM 13%	IND -13%	RE 20%	FIN -10%	HC -14%	IT 21%	RE -26%	CD -1%	CS 18%	CS 16%	HC -12%	COMM 8%
RE -121%	COMM 11%	RE -18%	IND -59%	IT 9%	RE -28%	COMM 20%	RE -10%	COMM -14%	HC 2%	COMM -40%	IND 5%	FIN 12%	HC 16%	IT -22%	UTIL -19%

Single-Factor Investing (Momentum)

Another type of thematic investment is single-factor investing. In the world of investing, there are some well-known ways of investing. These are called 'factors'. The most common ones are momentum, value, growth, quality, volatility and yield.

Momentum, specifically, is very popular. There are hundreds of portfolios designed by various investment advisors which focus on selecting stocks with momentum.

TABLE 2.5 Momentum Performance vs Index

Year	Nifty 200 TR* Index	Nifty 200 Momentum 30 TR Index
2023	23.5%	41.7%
2022	3.7%	–5.5%
2021	27.5%	53.8%
2020	15.6%	20.0%
2019	8.7%	10.6%
2018	–1.0%	–1.7%
2017	33.4%	57.5%
2016	3.7%	9.6%
2015	–1.9%	10.9%
2014	35.5%	49.6%
2013	4.4%	12.9%
2012	31.6%	38.8%
2011	–27.0%	–16.1%
2010	14.2%	19.8%
2009	86.6%	69.3%
2008	–56.6%	–60.0%
2007	63.7%	100.8%
2006	34.6%	44.2%

* Total return, which includes price increase and dividends as well as any other corporate actions

There are many different ways of measuring momentum—12-month momentum, 6-month momentum, momentum adjusted for volatility, long-term momentum minus short-term momentum and so on.

Momentum, like all thematic investments, does not work all the time. In Table 2.5, you can see that it underperformed the regular index in 4 out of 18 years.

Conclusion: Best Performing Fund

Investment by theme or sector is more diversified and stable than investing in a single security. However, in the long run, the results tend to underperform the broad index. Also, the effort required to study and analyse the themes is significant and more than what is possible for a common investor.

Check Your Understanding

1. What is a thematic investment?
   a. Investment in a single security
   b. Investment in a broad index
   c. Investment based on a specific theme or sector
   d. Investment based on short-term trends
2. What is the first challenge with thematic investing?
   a. Adjusting your view about the theme
   b. Tracking the themes and selecting the right one
   c. Finding the right company to invest in
   d. Dealing with market volatility
3. What is momentum investing?
   a. Investment based on short-term price trends
   b. Investment in a single security
   c. Investment based on a specific theme or sector
   d. Investment in a broad index

Answers: 1–c, 2–b, 3–a

Market Timing

It is dangerous to make forecasts, especially about the future.

—Niels Bohr

THE 'EXPERTS' WHO APPEAR on TV and constantly make predictions about market moves don't seem to be deterred by the danger or the risk of being proved wrong. This noise in the media is the hardest noise to ignore in investing. The predictions broadcasted encourage investors to time the market.

The 'experts' appearing on TV channels will have you believe that they can predict the future and guide you when to invest and when not to invest in the market. The simplest version of this advice is to avoid investing in the markets when the markets are down significantly. Let us look at the evidence. We have used the data from the US markets, as the history of market returns is available there for a longer period. In Figure 2.5, we see the next year return of S&P 500 index against the current year return. Left to right, we have marked the return each year, and top to bottom, we have marked the return in the following year. The dotted line is the trend line. Figure 2.5 shows us that the trend line is flat. There is no evidence that poor returns follow a year of poor returns.

FIGURE 2.5 S&P 500 Current Return vs Next Year Return

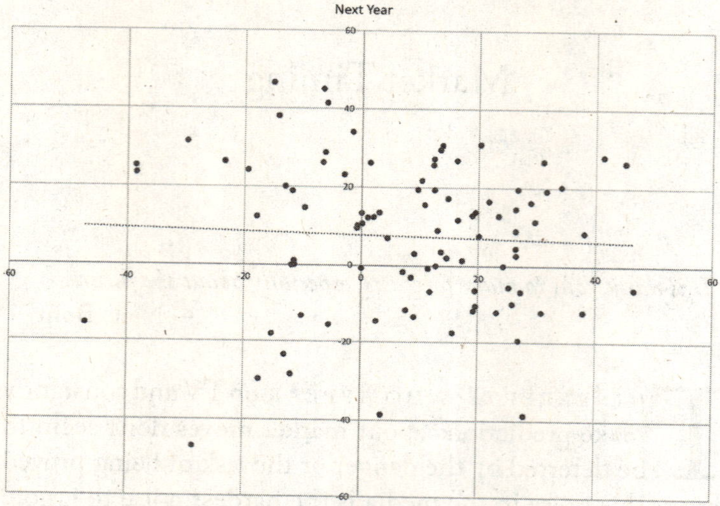

To further evaluate market timing, let us look at the return in the next five years following a good or bad year. In Figure 2.6, we can see the return of the current year plotted against the return achieved in the next five years. Interestingly, we see a negative trend—this means that poorer returns mean better returns in the next 5 years. Out of 24 years in which the returns were negative for S&P 500, only in 2 cases were the returns negative in the next 5 years.

This validates the advice given by Warren Buffett, 'Be fearful when others are greedy, and be greedy when others are fearful.' The returns following low-return years are higher than the returns following high-return years.

FIGURE 2.6 S&P 500 Return vs Next 5-Year Return

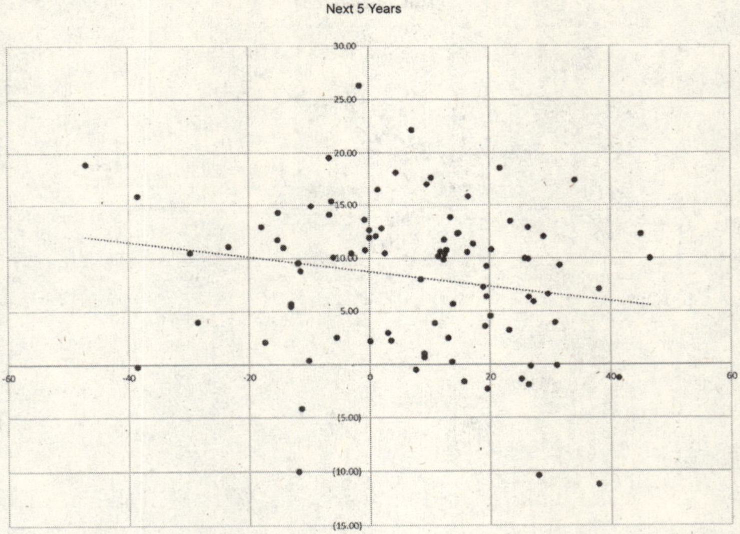

The extension of trends is the simplest type of advice that is given. Many gurus spout more convincing rationale. They share loads of facts to state that the economy is slowing down and hence investing in the stock market is not a good idea. Let us examine the linkage of GDP growth and stock market return. Figure 2.7 shows that there is very little connection between the GDP growth and stock market return. The chart looks like a scatter plot with no real pattern. In general, the trend line shows an upward slope which means higher GDP growth rate results in higher stock market returns. But just assessing GDP growth rate, even if you could assess it accurately, is not sufficient to predict stock market returns.

FIGURE 2.7 Market Return vs GDP

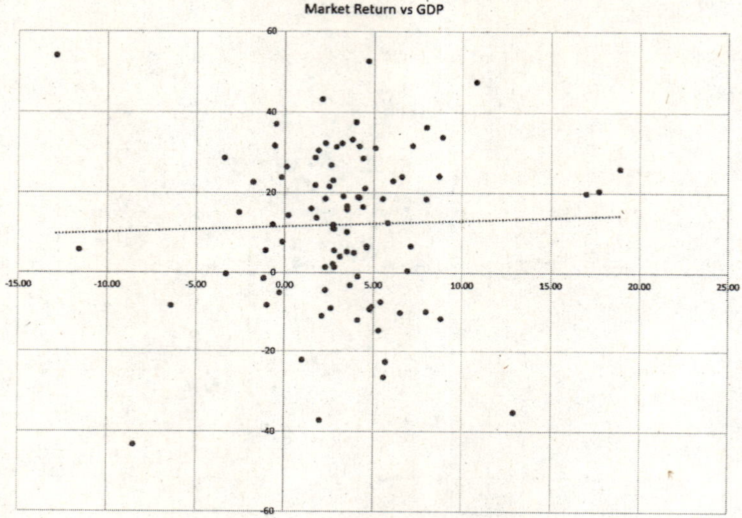

Thus we see that it is not easy to predict when the markets will go up or down. But what if you had a magic formula and you could know on which day the markets would be the lowest every year? Would you be significantly better off than investing regularly every month, no matter whether the markets were high or low? This issue is emotionally so difficult for people to understand that in every cycle of the stock market we see the same thing—a large number of people buy stocks when markets are near the top and sell them when they are close to the bottom. In the process, they end up making losses, though the markets produce good returns overall.

Let us assume there are two investors—one who buys stocks worth ₹10,000 every month on the first of the month, and the other who is somehow able to get the best possible outcome of buying at the lowest price of the year. So the second investor invests the whole amount of ₹1,20,000 every year at the lowest price of the year. Over an investment period of 30 years, how big a difference do you think this will produce in their total portfolio value? The results are given in Table 2.6.

TABLE 2.6 Market Timing Impact

	Stable Investor	**Lucky Investor**
Invest	On 1st of every month	On the day of the lowest price in the year
Amount	10,000 per month, 1,20,000 per year	1,20,000 per year
Period	1994-2023	1994-2023
Total invested amount	36,00,000	36,00,000
Portfolio value at the end	3,36,81,497	4,06,76,852
Impact of market timing		20.8%

So over a period of 30 years, the perfectly lucky investor only outperforms the disciplined investor by 13.7%. Do you believe you will be able to time the market perfectly every year? It is just not worth all the anxiety trying to time the market for a little bit of extra return.

Expert Predictions

If you are still not convinced about the futility of trying to predict future returns, let me summarize the results of a fascinating study conducted by Philip E. Tetlock. Tetlock is the Annenberg University Professor at the University of Pennsylvania. From 1984 to 2003, he collected forecasts made by experts like professors, journalists, political commentators and senior government functionaries. He also collected forecasts made by college students who were not experts in the field. The study collected nearly 28,000 predictions about the future and found that the forecasters barely outperformed the control group of college students. More interesting was the finding that the more confident the expert was, the less accurate they proved to be. When you are an expert on TV or newspaper, you need to present your predictions with confidence according to P.E. Tetlock in *Expert Political Judgement: How Good Is It? How Can We Know?*. This stands true to the maxim, 'Often wrong, never in doubt.'

Another anecdote related in the book is about an experiment in which a rat was put in a maze in which food was put randomly on one side 60% of the time and on the other side 40% of the time. The rat quickly realized that one side was better and always went to that side resulting in a success rate of 60%. The same experiment was repeated with Yale undergraduate students. Ivy League undergrads could not settle simply for a 60% success rate, so they tried to find a pattern to pick the right or left side. There was no pattern. As a result, the success rate for the undergraduates was only 52%. The more of an expert we are, the higher the tendency to see patterns where none exist.

Conclusion

It is tempting to follow the herd and sell when everyone is selling and buy when everyone is buying. The evidence does not support the simple view that poor returns or even poor economic growth mean poor returns in the future. Nor do the experts on the TV or social media have any better ability to predict the market returns. Even the benefit, if you could time the market perfectly, is small compared to the overall growth of the equity markets over long periods of time. Hence stay invested instead of trying to time the market.

Check Your Understanding

1. What does Figure 2.7 show about market timing?
   a. Poor returns follow poor returns
   b. Good returns follow good returns
   c. Difficult to predict a trend in returns
   d. The S&P 500 index is consistently volatile
2. What is the negative trend seen in Figure 2.6?
   a. Poorer returns mean better returns in the next 5 years
   b. Better returns mean higher returns in the next 5 years
   c. The market returns are unpredictable
   d. The market returns are consistently negative
3. What is the main emotional issue for people with respect to market timing?
   a. Fear of missing out on potential gains
   b. Fear of losing money in a downturn
   c. Difficulty in understanding market trends
   d. Inability to access the necessary data

Answers: 1–c, 2–a, 3–a

Separate Savings Pools for Each Goal

Our friend, Chanchal Kumar, has many things he wants to achieve in life—buy a home in 3 years, pay for the foreign education of his two children and save for a comfortable retirement. He has done some reading and started saving for his retirement using a well-diversified portfolio. For buying a house, he has kept aside ₹9 lakh in a bank fixed deposit. And now to save for his children's education, he is thinking of buying some safe investment since he does not want to take a risk with his children's future. Does his plan sound right to you?

THIS IS A COMMON STYLE of planning for many people. They create separate savings pools for each of their goals. If they are sophisticated or advised by a good financial advisor, then each of the pool will have proper asset allocation to meet the specific goal it has for itself. Is that the best approach?

The benefit of separate savings pools is that there is a sense of clarity. Each pool represents your efforts towards a specific goal. The emotional motivation is stronger as each of the goals is real and meaningful to you.

The downsides are many more. When you separate your savings into multiple pools, you face many challenges. The biggest one is your ability to do a proper asset allocation. Let us take the case of the three goals of Chanchal Kumar.

Table 2.7 shows the monthly savings needed to secure each goal. You can estimate savings required for any goal by using the online tool made available at https://www.gulaq.com/estimating-savings-for-goal/.

TABLE 2.7 Separate and Combined Savings for Goals[10]

Goal	Time	Target Money	Monthly Savings Required (Separate Goals)	Monthly Savings Required (Joint Goal)
Buy Home	3 Years	10,00,000	25,261	48,993
Children's Education	10 Years	1,00,00,000	49,259	
Retirement	30 Years	4,00,00,000	11,802	
Total			**86,322**	**48,993**

Chanchal Kumar needs to invest for Goal 1 (buying a home) in the safest way possible, like the Gear 1 investment that we described in the previous chapter. But if he was to invest in a common pool for the three goals, then the corpus available for the three goals could allow him to follow higher risk and higher return strategies without the danger of falling short of the money required for the goals. Specifically, for these three goals, he would require a monthly saving of ₹48,993 or 44% less than the separate goals.

The first reason is that the savings are spread over a longer period. Early in your life, you will have many goals that you need to save for, so if you start saving for all the goals, you will need a large amount of savings, and as you grow older and accomplish some of your goals, the savings required will decline steadily. This will be the inverse of your earning power, which will continue to increase over the years as you become more established in your work. The other reason is that the risk of missing your target in a group of goals is lower than the risk of missing your target in any one goal. Let us imagine that you have to buy 3 things—a jacket, shoes and a suitcase. Let us say that the jacket costs ₹4,000–5,000, the shoes cost ₹3,000–4,000 and the suitcase costs ₹5,000–7,000. Now if you carried enough money for each item, you would need to carry ₹16,000. However, if you believed that not everything you want to buy will be the most expensive in the range you evaluate, then you need to carry only ₹15,000—on an average, the three things will cost only ₹14,000 and you have more than that.

The second challenge is of management. Chanchal Kumar has to manage three separate pools of investments, allocate money to each of the pools every month and track the performance of each pool. This is 3 times more time consuming than having a single pool.

And finally, the challenge of deciding where to withdraw from for every contingency is much harder. Let's say Chanchal Kumar has an urgent expense where he needs to withdraw ₹1,00,000 from his savings. Which of these investment pools will he use? Or conversely, let us say that he received a special bonus of ₹2,00,000 in his job. How does he invest it? How much should he put in each pool? These decisions are difficult for a common investor. A single savings pool makes the task much simpler.

Check Your Understanding

1. Which of the following are benefits of a single pool of savings compared with separate pools?
   i. A single pool requires lower monthly savings for the same assurance of achieving the goals
   ii. A single pool is easier to manage
   iii. A single pool makes it easy to track how much money you have for each goal

   a. i and ii
   b. i and iii
   c. ii and iii
   d. i, ii and iii

2. What is *not* a downside of having a separate pool of investment for each goal?
   a. You need more savings
   b. You can't do proper asset allocation
   c. You can't track progress of each goal separately
   d. It is difficult to manage

Answers: 1–a, 2–c

Part 3

Staying the Course

Measuring Performance

How do you know that your investments are working well? This is a question that appears simple but is very difficult to answer. Most people believe that their investments are doing well when they make profits and badly when they make losses. In addition, they look at only the returns and not at the risk they took to generate the returns.

Risk versus Return

Risk and return are two sides of the same coin. There is no return without taking some risk. Though the converse is not true—you can take a risk and not get enough return to compensate for it!

> Chanchal Kumar is comparing two funds. One fund gave a return of 12% over the last one year and the other fund gave a return of 10%. Chanchal Kumar prefers the first fund. Is he correct? Looking only at the return is like looking only at the physical beauty of your prospective partner or friend. Yes, beauty is important, but you have to understand the temperament of the person as well. There is more than one attribute that is important. Similarly, in an investment, it is important to understand return as well as risk. Chanchal Kumar should be asking about the riskiness of each fund.

Two common ways to understand risk are:

1. To understand the Maximum Draw Down (MDD) of the investment.
2. To understand the standard deviation of the returns.

MDD represents the maximum money you could lose if you invested in a particular security. It is measured by looking at the historical returns of the product and measuring the maximum loss that any investor suffered in it, from the highest to the subsequent lowest point.

Standard deviation is a term from statistics. You can understand it as a measure of how much the return can vary from period to period.

Information Ratio is a concept which measures the signal-to-noise ratio in an investment. Signal is the average return and noise is the standard deviation of that return over a period of time.

Here is an example in Table 3.1. Let's say you are comparing, Fund A, which gave a return of 8% on an average for the past 5 years, and Fund B, which gave a return of 12% on an average for the past 5 years. Which one is better?

When we look at the annual returns, we see that they vary a lot—between 5.8% and 11.6% for Fund A and between 5.4% and 22.9% for Fund B. The variation for Fund B is much more than for Fund A. Investors use the ratio of return over risk to compare the attractiveness of a fund. In our example, in Table 3.1, the Information Ratio of Fund A is 3.4% which is twice as that of Fund B, which is 1.7%. Even though the return for Fund A is lower and adjusted for risk, Fund A is a better investment.

Separating Skill and Luck

Profit or loss is a combination of the skill of the investor and the underlying risk of the investment. If you are investing in a fixed deposit in a bank, it is highly unlikely

TABLE 3.1 Understanding Risk and Return

Year	Fund A	Fund B
Year 1	10.2%	18.7%
Year 2	6.0%	6.1%
Year 3	5.8%	5.4%
Year 4	6.7%	8.0%
Year 5	11.6%	22.9%
Average	8.1%	12.2%
Standard Deviation	2.4%	7.2%
Information Ratio	3.4%	1.7%

that you will make a loss. Does that mean you are a great investor? On the other hand, if you invest in stock markets, it is equally impossible to always have a profitable year. Legendary investor Warren Buffett, in 56 years of investing, had 10 years with negative returns—including 1973, when he lost 48.7% of the portfolio value. Does that mean Warren Buffett is not a great investor?

The secret to measuring performance is to separate the two components—skill of the investor and the underlying risk of the investment. This is done by using a proper benchmark for the investment. We discussed benchmark earlier in this book, in the section 'Side Bar: Benchmark'.

In the case of Warren Buffett, since he invests mostly in companies in the US, a proper comparison would be to use the US market index S&P 500. This represents the top 500 companies in the US stock market. Compared with the S&P 500, Warren Buffett produced nearly twice the returns over the period 1965 to 2022. S&P 500 produced a return of 9.8% whereas Warren Buffett (via Berkshire Hathaway) produced a return of 19.8%. This comparison shows the skill of the investor. Please note that we used a benchmark (S&P 500) to review the performance objectively.

Similarly, for investments in a fixed deposit, we would compare them to an index of fixed deposit returns. When we invest in a blended fashion with some investments in stocks and some in debt, we need to combine the stock index with the debt index in the same proportion as the investment, to get the benchmark index.

The financial industry does not make it easy to measure performance in this manner. Even though SEBI requires every individual mutual fund to identify a benchmark, the overall portfolio that you hold does not have a benchmark. For the convenience of investors, on gulaq.com, we provide a basic facility to measure benchmark performance between any two dates as well as for any combination of asset allocation.

Check Your Understanding

1. If you have an option of investing in Fund A, with an average return of 10% and standard deviation of 5%, and Fund B, with an average return of 15% and a standard deviation of 10%, which one would you pick?
   a. Fund A
   b. Fund B
   c. 50% in Fund A, 50% in Fund B
2. If your portfolio of stocks grew by 25% while the Nifty Index went up by 28% in the same year, would you think you invested skilfully?
   a. Yes
   b. No
   c. Can't say
3. If your portfolio lost 4%, would you say that you are not a skilled investor?
   a. Yes
   b. No
   c. Can't say

Answers: 1–a, 2–c, 3–c

Rebalancing

'REBALANCING' IS A WORD we hear when we go for servicing our car. It means to move around the tyres and adjust the suspension so that any impact of uneven usage of tyres is fixed. In investment, rebalancing means to bring your asset allocation to the desired or target levels.

Let's say that you start with a 60% equity and 40% debt allocation. After some good years, when the equity markets have gone up 50% and debt markets have returned 10%, your allocation will become 67% equity and 33% debt. Now comes the hardest part. To be a good investor, you must sell some equity holdings and buy debt.

You will protest—why should I sell equity right after it has gone up 50% and buy debt holdings which have only given me 10% return? It is equal to selling my wins and buying my losses. Does it make any sense?

As mentioned earlier, the famous investor Warren Buffett said, 'Be fearful when others are greedy, and greedy when others are fearful.' Rebalancing is a disciplined way of adhering to this advice.

Investors should rebalance their portfolio to the desired allocation at least once a year. In Figure 3.1 you can see the difference between a rebalanced portfolio and a portfolio that was not rebalanced. Rebalancing every year means that at the end of every year the portfolio is brought back to the target allocation of 60%–40% (or whatever was the target you had started with). If the equity part outperformed the debt part, then you should sell some of the equity portfolio and invest in the debt portfolio.

FIGURE 3.1 Impact of Rebalancing

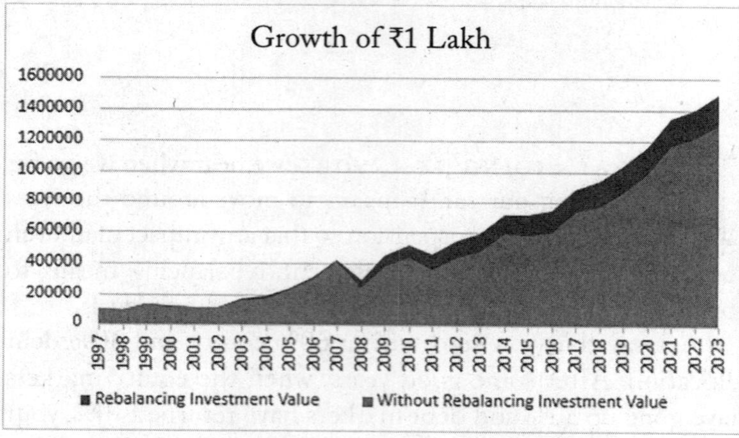

Check Your Understanding

1. What is the meaning of rebalancing an investment?
   a. Buying different securities based on their performance
   b. Bringing back your asset allocation to the desired levels
   c. Buying more equity holdings to increase your returns
   d. Buying better stocks and selling poor performers
2. How often should investors rebalance their portfolio?
   a. Once every two years
   b. Once every three years
   c. At least once a year and more often if required
   d. It depends on the market conditions

Answers: 1–b, 2–c

Adjusting Your Goals

A PART OF REBALANCING IS also to look at the goals and expectations you have. The timing of using your savings can have a big impact on your savings plan. Table 3.2 shows the outcome for an investor over 10 years. The returns are 15% every year, except one year when they go down to –15%. In one case, that year comes right at the beginning of the period and in the other case, the year with –15% return comes at the end. Notice that the total savings at the end of the 10-year period are the same. It did not matter when the bad year occurred.

TABLE 3.2 Timing Effect of Negative Return

	Case-1			Case-2		
Year	**Saving**	**Return**	**Ending Saving**	**Saving**	**Return**	**Ending Saving**
1	10,00,000	–15%	8,50,000	10,00,000	15%	11,50,000
2	8,50,000	15%	9,77,500	11,50,000	15%	13,22,500
3	9,77,500	15%	11,24,125	13,22,500	15%	15,20,875
4	11,24,125	15%	12,32,744	15,20,875	15%	17,49,007
5	12,92,745	15%	14,86,655	17,49,006	15%	20,11,357
6	14,85,655	15%	17,09,654	20,11,357	15%	23,13,061
7	17,09,654	15%	19,66,102	23,13,061	15%	26,60,020
8	19,56,102	15%	22,61,017	26,60,020	15%	30,59,023
9	22,61,017	15%	26,00,169	30,59,023	15%	35,17,876
10	26,00,169	15%	29,90,195	35,17,876	15%	29,90,195

Let us change the scenario to where the investor was withdrawing ₹1 lakh every year. The results are very different now. In this case, the investor ends up with much less money if the –15% year occurs early.

This is due to the effect of compounding. The way to address this is to also look at your expenses and expectations, besides savings, investments and returns. If the returns are lower than targeted, then reduce your expectations and expenses during that period. Skip some of the expenses till the times are better. On the other hand, if the returns are good, you can spend a bit more without compromising your outcome.

TABLE 3.3 Timing Effect of Expenses

	Case-1				Case-2			
Year	**Saving**	**Return**	**Spending**	**Ending Savings**	**Saving**	**Return**	**Spending**	**Ending Savings**
1	10,00,000	-15%	1,00,000	7,50,000	10,00,000	15%	1,00,000	10,50,000
2	7,50,000	15%	1,00,000	7,62,500	11,50,000	15%	1,00,000	11,07,500
3	7,62,500	15%	1,00,000	7,76,875	13,22,500	15%	1,00,000	11,73,625
4	7,76,875	15%	1,00,000	7,93,406	15,20,875	15%	1,00,000	12,49,669
5	7,93,406	15%	1,00,000	8,12,417	17,49,006	15%	1,00,000	13,37,119
6	8,12,417	15%	1,00,000	8,34,280	20,11,357	15%	1,00,000	14,37,687
7	8,34,280	15%	1,00,000	8,59,422	23,13,061	15%	1,00,000	15,53,340
8	8,59,422	15%	1,00,000	8,88,335	2,66,60,020	15%	1,00,000	16,86,341
9	8,88,335	15%	1,00,000	9,21,585	30,59,023	15%	1,00,000	18,39,292
10	9,21,585	15%	1,00,000	9,59,823	35,17,876	15%	1,00,000	14,63,398

When to Call Quits

It is possible to make money—and a great deal of money—in the stock market. But it can't be done overnight or by haphazard buying and selling. The big profits go to the intelligent, careful and patient investor, not to the reckless and overeager speculator.

—J. Paul Getty

INNUMERABLE BOOKS HAVE BEEN written about the psychology of investing. A lot of investors fall prey to the two emotions—greed and fear—which are the biggest destroyer of returns.

In a bull market, everyone seems to be minting money and the returns appear so good that greed takes over. Throwing a systematic plan to the wind, investors make very speculative investments based on rumours and 'sure tips'. In a downturn, the opposite happens. People lose their nerve and sell at the bottom of the market, losing all the upside in the process. This is the emotional aspect of investing. No matter how much you understand the underlying investment principles, emotions overrule logic most of the time.

It is better to develop a method after a careful study of all the elements and to not change course in between if the returns are within the range of expected returns.

For many investors, the problem is not about holding investments patiently. The problem is the decision to exit. Kahneman and Tversky, whom I mentioned earlier, discovered the 'endowment effect'. This is the irrational feeling in which the value of things increases in your mind as soon as you acquire them. That is, emotionally, people value things more when they own them than when they don't own them.

In an experiment, people were given either $2 cash or a lottery ticket costing $2. After some time, the ones with lottery tickets were offered $2 to buy them back, but they refused. Surprisingly, when the ones with $2 were offered a lottery ticket for $2, they also refused. Due to the endowment effect, the value of the lottery ticket was more than $2 for those who had it and less than $2 for those who did not.

This effect is very commonly visible in stock investing. Once someone buys a stock, they are extremely averse to selling it at a price lower than their purchase price because they believe it is worth more than what they paid for it. This results in people holding their stocks for longer periods than necessary, resulting in large losses.

> I saw this firsthand in a dramatic way in the crash of 2000. I was a partner in a firm called Mitchell Madison Group, which was acquired by a company that eventually rebranded itself as 'marchFirst'. Bob Bernard was the CEO and owned nearly a billion dollars' worth (at its peak) of stock. In the crash, the stock price of the company started falling from its peak of $80. Bob not only did not sell any stock but borrowed money against his stock for other investments. As a result, he ended up with nothing as the company's stock kept falling and eventually the company declared bankruptcy. At every point, Bob thought that the stock was worth much more than the current market price. It was sad and poignant to watch someone lose a billion dollars in a few months. In those days, a billion dollars was still a lot of money to lose!

Whenever you make an investment, you should know the Maximum Draw Down (MDD) or the maximum loss that the investment can suffer. Set a rigid stop loss at the MDD level or slightly beyond that. Let's say that the MDD of an investment is 20%. Set the stop loss at 25%. If the investment loses 25%, you simply exit. The assumptions and past performance are no longer applicable as the loss has been larger than anything seen in the past. This MDD can also be measured in terms of absolute return and also as underperformance relative to the market. For example, you may set a guideline that while a stock may lose more than 50% of its value, it should not underperform the broad market index by more than 10%.

If you are investing with a fund or an investment advisor, then it is reasonable to look at the MDD at the overall portfolio level. This is a question you must ask and get answered before you invest. Typically, a diversified portfolio of stocks will have a lower MDD compared to a single stock. The historical performance of absolute returns and relative returns can help you set the right level of monitoring thresholds.

Holding on beyond what is reasonable based on historical performance is not a sign of patience, it is a sign of lack of discipline and emotional attachment to a decision that has gone bad.

If you have invested in a fund, you must also compare its performance with the benchmark index. If your fund has performed poorly but better than the index, then you can have more confidence in holding on to the investment.

This approach is only applicable to specific investments. On an overall basis, you must stay invested. If you exit when the markets are down and stay out of the markets as the markets recover, then you will end up selling at the bottom and then losing a lot of potential gain. We had discussed this question in more detail in the section 'Market Timing'.

Check Your Understanding

1. What emotions do investors often fall prey to?
   a. Greed and impatience
   b. Fear and impatience
   c. Greed and fear
   d. None of the above
2. Why do investors hold on to losing stocks?
   a. They believe the stock is worth more than the current market price
   b. They are afraid of selling at a loss
   c. They are emotionally attached to the decision that has gone bad
   d. All of the above
3. What is the endowment effect?
   a. People value a thing more when they don't own it
   b. People value a thing more when they own it
   c. People value a thing the same, whether they own it or not
   d. None of the above
4. What is Maximum Draw Down (MDD)?
   a. The maximum return that an investment can earn
   b. The maximum loss that an investment can suffer
   c. The maximum amount of money an investor can invest in a particular stock
   d. None of the above

Answers: 1–c, 2–d, 3–b, 4–b

Tax Harvesting

LOSSES CAN ALSO BE useful if used properly in an investment strategy. There is a big difference in the long-term and short-term tax rate. In the financial year (FY) 2023–24, for equities and equity-oriented mutual funds, the long-term capital gains tax was 10% whereas the short-term capital gains tax was 15%. For this purpose, 'short-term' was defined as a period of one year or less and 'long-term' as a period of more than one year. When you hold a portfolio of investments, it is inevitable that some investments will do better than others. If you have some investments which are making a loss, then you may benefit by selling such stocks before the year is over. This would generate short-term capital loss. This can be used to offset short-term or long-term capital gains.

So, at the end of a financial year, an investor can sell a set of loss-making investments and profit-making investments with the same amount of profits as the booked losses. The net tax on such investments would be zero. In India, there is no restriction on purchasing the same security immediately after selling it. So the investor can buy the security again immediately. The higher cost of purchase at that time would reduce future taxes as well.

This activity is called 'Tax Harvesting'. It is well within the income tax laws and beneficial to investors.

In addition, there is another long-term capital gains tax benefit. Up to ₹1 lakh of long-term capital gains are exempt from tax, so an investment plan should capture this tax benefit.

Check Your Understanding

1. At the start of the year, an investor bought ₹100,000 worth of stock A, B and C each. Just before the end of the year, stock A is worth ₹90,000, stock B is worth ₹120,000 and stock C is worth ₹140,000. The investor does not believe that stock A is a good investment anymore. What is the best tax harvesting strategy?
   a. Sell stock A. Recognize capital loss and carry it forward
   b. Sell stock A and stock B. This reduces taxable profit from ₹20,000 to ₹10,000
   c. Sell stock A and half of stock B. This reduces taxes to zero
2. Is it legal to do tax harvesting in India?
   a. Yes, but only on a large scale
   b. Yes, in all cases
   c. No, it is considered tax evasion

Answers: 1–c, 2–b

PART 4

Taking It Further

Congratulations on making it so far in this book. By now you have learnt everything you need to know to outperform a vast majority of investors, while spending very little effort. This is what almost everyone should do. Assess your goals, set a savings plan, allocate assets, select the right investment products and watch your portfolio grow. But if you want to go deeper and learn how to do the actual stock picking yourself, then this section is for you.

The treatment of the subject here is brief—it is more to provide a preview of how some of the most sophisticated investors build their portfolios.

Multifactor Models

When you think of famous investors, what names come to your mind? For most people, it is names like Warren Buffett and Rakesh Jhunjhunwala. Successful investors study the companies in depth and understand the prospects of the business. They review the management strength, the competitive landscape and the strength of the products and services of the company. They understand the revenue and margin trends and then make an investment decision. This type of investment is called 'Fundamental Research'. I am not an expert in this area and will not be elaborating on it. There are innumerable books about this method.

There is another way to build an investment portfolio. It relies on quantitative analysis of historical data to assess how to build a portfolio. The key difference is that a Fundamental Analyst makes an assessment based on the evaluation and (human) judgement of many pieces of historical information as well as its extrapolation into the future, while a Quantitative Analyst focuses on assessing potential performance based on historical data and patterns that can be discerned in them.

Each historical data element that can provide insight into future performance is called a 'factor'. The simplest factor is momentum. It means that if a stock has had a recent price increase—meaning its price has momentum—then it is likely to do well. This is the Momentum Factor. Similarly, you can have a Value Factor—here the assumption is that stocks which are priced cheaply relative to their earnings capability will increase in price. Growth Factor says that companies whose revenue has been increasing rapidly will continue to grow.

A multifactor model assesses dozens, if not hundreds, of such factors. At my firm, Estee, we test hundreds of factors to assess their ability to predict future performance. For each factor, we calculate the value for each stock and then rank it based on the factor. For momentum, we may measure the price change in the past 12 months and then rank the companies in order of the rate of change of price. The assumption is that the stocks with the highest increase will continue to outperform the stocks which have the lowest price increase. Many people take the top 20% of the companies on every factor. This process is also called a Single Factor Model.

We can take several factors, assign weights to each factor and build an overall portfolio. How much importance or weight is given to each factor is dependent on the effectiveness of that factor. This will become a Multifactor Model.

Here are the descriptions of major types of factors that are considered in investment analysis.

Price Momentum

Price change is used both to assess what trends will continue as well as what trends are likely to reverse. A long-term trend (e.g., 9 months) may indicate that the price will continue to rise, but a short-term trend (e.g., one month) might indicate that the price may reverse.

Value

A company's business value is its intrinsic ability to generate earnings. One common measure is the price to earnings (P/E) ratio. If a ₹1,000 crore market capitalization company generates ₹100 crore profit a year, then it has a P/E ratio of 10. Another company with same market capitalization of ₹1,000 crore but earnings of ₹200 crore will have a P/E ratio of 5. The assumption is that the company with the lower P/E ratio will appreciate in value.

There are many measures of value used for Value Factor, for example, price to cash flow, price to earnings before non-cash expenses, book value versus market value and so on.

Growth

For the past 20 years, a large part of the global market appreciation has come from new companies like Facebook, Amazon, Google, Apple and Netflix. These businesses have grown consistently in revenue and earnings over a long period. Investing in such companies is 'growth investing'. The measures of growth are earnings growth, revenue growth and cash flow growth. Many such companies are not 'value' companies as they have high P/E ratios.

Quality

Investors also assess the ratio of earnings with actual cash generated. Sometimes accruals can hide the problems of receivables in a company's growth, so companies where earnings and cash flow are growing are considered better. Also, the level of debt and balance sheet strength are factors considered in the quality of earnings.

Low Volatility

This measures stability and robustness of earnings. A company which grows at a consistent rate year after year is considered better than a company which grows erratically, though overall it may grow the same amount over a long period of time.

Technical Indicators

A subcategory of factors are technical indicators. These are indicators that use only price and volume of the stock transactions on the stock exchange. The patterns that are formed by the price and volume are considered capable of predicting future returns.

Investor Holding

Details of which investors are buying or selling the stock can also reveal the future direction of the stock price. If highly knowledgeable institutional investors are accumulating a stock, then it is considered a positive sign. Also, the trades of 'insiders'—management, promoters and directors—are also good indicators as they are supposed to know more about the company's prospects than the average investor. So their actions reveal their confidence about the direction of the price of the stock.

Index Participation

We talked about active versus passive investments. The world is increasingly moving towards passive investments. As the size of passive investment funds grows, it has an impact on stocks which are a part of major indices. It is a simple matter of demand and supply. As the money to be deployed in index funds grows, there is a higher demand for stocks which are a part of the index. This results in the increase of the price of these stocks. So knowing which index a stock is a part of and whether it is joining or leaving an index is important in determining its price movement.

This is not meant to be an exhaustive list—a lot has been written about investment factors. You can know more about this by reading the work of Fama and French (mentioned earlier) and many other academic researchers.

Macro Environment

All businesses operate in a political and economic environment. Factors like interest rates, inflation, cost of energy, GDP growth rate, currency exchange rate and, above all, demographics, have very significant impact on business performance.

Each of the factors discussed so far may behave differently in different macro environments.

Check Your Understanding

1. What is Fundamental Research?
    a. Quantitative analysis of historical data to assess how to build a portfolio
    b. Analysis of management strength, competitive landscape and products and services of a company to make investment decisions
    c. A sub-category of factors using only price and volume action of the stock in exchange trading
    d. An analysis of which investors are buying or selling the stock to reveal the future direction of the stock price
2. Which of the following is a type of factor that is considered in investment analysis?
    a. Technical indicators
    b. Index participation
    c. Investor holding
    d. All of the above
3. Which of the following is an example of a Value Factor?
    a. Revenue growth
    b. Cash flow growth

   c. PE Ratio
   d. Stability of earnings
4. What is volatility?
   a. A measure of stability and robustness of earnings
   b. An analysis of which investors are buying or selling the stock to reveal the future direction of the stock price
   c. A sub-category of factors using only price and volume action of the stock in exchange trading
   d. A measure of growth in revenue and earnings over a long period of time

Answers: 1–b, 2–d, 3–c, 4–a

Building a Portfolio

Selecting a Universe

When you apply multifactor models on some selected set of securities, these securities are called your investment universe. You can focus on the top 50 companies in India—then your universe will be Nifty 50. Or you could expand your investment universe to the top 100 or 500 companies. Then your universe will be Nifty 100 or Nifty 500, respectively. It is important to select the appropriate universe for your investment objectives. For example, many experienced investors generate higher returns by investing in small cap companies. This means that their universe is Nifty 500 or even smaller companies. If you invest only in Nifty 50 companies, then you should not compare your returns directly with Nifty 500 returns.

Scoring Securities on Factors

Once you have scored all your stocks in your selected universe on each of the factors you consider relevant, you have to convert the scores into a standardized (or normalized) figure to be able to use it for your investment portfolio. You can standardize the scores to be within a particular range. For example, if you are measuring the price change in the last six months, it may range from –30% to +40% with an average of 5%. This can be converted (i.e., normalized) into a number between –1 and 1. There are many ways of normalizing scores, but the objective is always the same—to bring widely different numbers within a common range. This makes it easier to process them.

Normalized scores are then combined together. You can assign weights to the individual normalized scores based on the strength of their ability to predict future returns. The ability of each factor to predict future returns is notoriously unstable. So some technical experts select the top few factors and give equal weight to them.

The combined score is then used to build a portfolio. Again, there are many ways of doing this. You can select the top score companies and give equal weight to them. Or you can give them weights according to the score (higher the score, higher the weight).

Assigning Weights to Securities

In the previous section, we learnt how to assess the attractiveness of a business by looking at various factors. After you have done the work of assessing each of the securities, you still have to create a portfolio. Creating a portfolio means that you have to decide how much of each security you will buy in your portfolio.

Earlier, in Part 1, we learnt about building a simple investment plan using just debt products and an index fund. An index fund holds the securities in a fixed ratio. For example, Nifty 50 has the top 50 companies in the ratio of free-float market capitalization. When you are building a portfolio, you may assign weights to each security which are different from the benchmark weights. For example, Reliance may have a 10% weight in the Nifty 500 index, but in your portfolio, you may assign it a weight which is more than 10% or less than 10%. This is called overweighting or underweighting a security.

The factor scores you assigned can help you assign weights to different securities. There are two very different methods to assign weights.

The first method is to adjust the weight of the security based on the attractiveness of the security. Overweight the securities which have a high score and underweight the securities which have a low score. In a portfolio like this, you hold a position in every one of the securities in the universe. But they are in a ratio different from the index.

The second method assigns absolute weights based on the score itself. In this method, no attention is paid to the weight of the securities in the index. Higher the score of the securities, higher is the weight they get. In this method, the final weight of the security in the portfolio can be very different from its weight in the index.

Backtesting and Overfitting

The factors you choose and the weights you assign to them will depend on how they perform in your backtest. Backtest means that you apply actual market data or historical data on the model you developed. You should test your model for a long enough period to have confidence that the model will work in all kinds of market scenarios. Many an investor has been burnt applying a model that worked beautifully for twelve months, only to discover that it does not work any more in the future. So you must test your model over a long period of time, ideally through two complete economic cycles of rising and falling economic growth, which is about 15 years.

When you test your model over 15 years, there is a risk of overfitting. The more factors you use and the more complex weighting and normalization mechanism you use, you will find a very specific combination which works for your specific period of backtest. But it may not work for another period. This is called overfitting. Overfitting is the bane of quant (quantitative) investors. It is very difficult to avoid and even harder to overcome.

There are some methods by which you can reduce the impact of overfitting. One method is to use a holdout period. When you are backtesting, keep some historical data (say, of the last 6 months) separate. Do not use it during the factor selection and weight assignment process. Once your model is fully ready, test it on this holdout period. The performance in the holdout period should be similar to the historical backtest period.

Another method is to see the performance year by year in the backtest period. Choose the method which produces lower variations year to year for the same overall performance. A consistent and stable performer is better than a method that produces spectacular highs and lows.

Tracking Error

The decision of assigning weights has a big impact on the tracking error of the portfolio. The more freedom you use in assigning weights which are different from the index weight, the higher is the tracking error that will result. Many professional investors prefer the first method described earlier.

One dimension of risk measurement is market cap exposure. If you are selecting only small cap stocks, then it is possible that your returns will be better, but it is also true that you are taking more risk than a market cap balanced portfolio.

There are other measures of risk control that a professional manager would take. The difference of sector exposure between the benchmark index and the portfolio gives an indication of how much risk you are taking in different sectors. An investor who only invests in technology stocks takes a large amount of risk in sector exposure.

Attribution Analysis

Professional investors track how their investment decisions are working in the market. They are not satisfied by looking at the overall market return—that is the end result. While it is important to know the end result, the first step is to measure the difference between the benchmark return and the portfolio return. This helps to understand whether your selections contributed anything to the return available from the benchmark index.

The return is further broken down between sectors, market cap and factor exposure. These break ups help you understand how much of the return came from exposure to a particular sector or market cap segment. The factor exposure analysis tells you how much of the return came due to picking of some standard factors like momentum or value.

The maths involved in calculating attribution is complicated and is available through market analysis tools like the ones provided by organizations like Bloomberg, Barra and Morningstar.

Check Your Understanding

1. What is the purpose of normalizing scores in stock investment portfolios?
   a. To get widely different numbers to fit in the same range
   b. To make it harder to combine them
   c. To make the scores more volatile
   d. To make the scores more predictable

2. How do investors weigh individual scores in their portfolio?
   a. By how confident they are about its ability to predict future returns
   b. By the number of companies with the same score
   c. By the size of the company
   d. By the number of shares owned
3. How can investors convert their combined score into a portfolio?
   a. By selecting the top scored companies and equal weighting them
   b. By giving them weight according to the score
   c. Both methods are used
   d. None of the above
4. Which of the following is *not* a factor that should be considered when selecting an investment universe?
   a. The size of the universe
   b. The liquidity of the securities in the universe
   c. The number of factors to be used
   d. The ability of the factors to predict future returns
   e. The volatility of the securities in the universe
5. Which of the following is *not* a method to assign weights to securities in a multifactor model?
   a. Equal weighting
   b. Attractiveness weighting
   c. Absolute weighting
   d. Index weighting
   e. Backtesting weighting
6. Which of the following statements is *true* about tracking error?
   a. It is a measure of how closely a portfolio tracks its benchmark index
   b. The higher the tracking error, the more closely does the portfolio track its benchmark index

c. The tracking error can be reduced by increasing the number of factors used in the multifactor model
d. The tracking error can be reduced by increasing the number of securities in the portfolio

7. Which of the following is *not* a measure of risk control that a professional manager would monitor?
   a. Sector exposure
   b. Market cap exposure
   c. Tracking error
   d. Attribution analysis

Answers: 1–a, 2–a, 3–c, 4–c, 5–e, 6–a, 7–d

Implementing Your Portfolio

Once you have a model that you have backtested and want to implement, you still have the challenge of implementing it in the actual stock market. The backtests on historical data make some assumptions. For example, they assume that you will be able to buy or sell at the closing price of the day. Or that the price at which they evaluate the portfolio is the price at which you will actually be able to transact. These assumptions are not exactly correct, and the variations in the transacted prices create a difference between the backtested results and the realized returns.

Implementation Shortfall

The closing price, based on which almost all the analysis is done, is not really available in the market at any time. In the stock exchange, the closing price is calculated by taking a volume-weighted average of prices over the last 30 minutes of trading. It is impossible to get exactly that price in an actual transaction.

Typically, the portfolio is scored with prices at a given point. Orders are generated and executed in the market at slightly different prices depending on how the markets move in the time between scoring and transacting. The difference between the price at which the order is given and the price at which it is executed is called the 'implementation shortfall'.

You must measure the total implementation shortfall and ensure that it is not taking away a lot of return.

Market Impact

Market impact is the phenomenon when your trading specifically impacts the market prices. At typical investment sizes this is not an issue as the markets are large and very liquid and the action of one individual investor hardly impacts the prices. However, if you are investing a lot of money or you are investing in stocks which do not have a high trading volume, then this can become an issue. You must know the average daily trading volume of the stock you want to transact in and compare it to your order size. This factor is usually relevant when your total order size is more than 5% of the daily market volume. Sometimes new investors buy stocks which have a short-term burst of activity. You must look at the longer-term pattern of how much trading takes place in the stock to assess if you would be able to sell your stock conveniently. SEBI and stock exchanges prohibit activity in which someone artificially increases the price and trading volume in a stock for a short period—called 'pump and dump'—but investors can help themselves by being aware of the normal volume of trading and avoiding any unusual increase in volume and prices.

Check Your Understanding

1. What impact does your trading have on stock market prices?
   a. No impact ever
   b. Sometimes it can have an impact depending on my volume and overall trading volume in the stock
   c. Always has an impact

2. What is 'implementation shortfall'?
   a. Mistakes made in trading
   b. Transaction costs
   c. Difference between the prices received by trading in the market and the prices when the decision was made to buy or sell the security

Answers: 1–b, 2–c

Appendix

We have provided many templates online to help you to implement the ideas shared in this book. These are available at www.gulaq.com/templates. We have described some of these templates in this section.

Estimating Annual Spend

THIS TEMPLATE ALLOWS YOU to estimate your annual spending and the total amount of savings you can make today using just 13 months of bank statements. There is no need to calculate a detailed budget or do detailed projections.

Here is the step-by-step process to get a good estimate of the expenses without collecting all the details of every single bill you paid or every transaction you made. You can find an online version at gulaq.com.

Step-by-Step Method to Estimate Expenses

1. We assume that you have a main bank account in which you deposit your salary and which is used for most of your expenses. Collect one year and one month (13 months) of statements for this account.
2. Now fill the balances for each month in the template.
3. You need to classify all outflows as 'asset purchase' (that is, 'investment') or 'expense'. This needs a little explanation. The money spent on an asset purchase or an investment will eventually come back when you liquidate the asset. For example, if you transfer money to your brokerage account, it is not an expense—it is an investment. Similarly, if you pay down payment on an apartment, it is not an expense, it is building an asset which one day you can sell and receive the value of in your bank account.

On the other hand, if you pay for a holiday, it is an expense. Since there are a lot more expenses than investments, you need to only identify investments and add them up for each month. Everything else is an expense.

4. Similarly, identify and classify inflows of money from investments as 'asset sale'. If you get your salary, it is a regular income; however, if you sell your motorbike and get money, that is 'asset sale'. Any return from an investment account—like dividends or interest—are also a partial asset sale.
5. Now you should have five numbers for each month:
    a. Balance at the start of the month (B1)
    b. Income (I)
    c. Asset purchase (P)
    d. Asset sale (S)
    e. Balance at the end of the month (B2)
6. You can determine the estimated expenses using these five numbers. You start with the balance at the start of the month (B1) and add income (I) and asset sale (S). This is the total inflow. Now you reduce it by asset purchase (P) and the balance at the end of the month (B2). The residual is your expense.
7. Expense E = B1 + I + S – B2 – P
8. Add the Expense (E) for every month for a year. This gives you a good estimate of your annual expenses.

The difference between your total income and total expense is your savings. The template is available at https://www.gulaq.com/estimating-savings/.

Buying or Renting a Home

This template compares the financial impact of buying or renting a house and the outcome in terms of end-of-period value.

The important variables that you need to input are as follows:

- Expected appreciation in the value of the house
- Total cost of purchase of the house
- Closing costs—registration, stamp duty, brokerage
- Down payment
- Home loan interest rate
- Tenure of home loan in years
- Initial rent (stated as a percentage of the value of the house)
- Rent appreciation
- Gear of investment (this determines the asset allocation and expected returns)

Once you select these parameters, the template calculates month-to-month cash flows and compares the final net value of your portfolio at the end of the loan period. The assumption is that you will invest the down payment as well as the additional money (difference between EMI and rent) into your investment portfolio. This template is available at https://www.gulaq.com/buying-home-vs-renting-house/.

Retirement Planning

THIS TEMPLATE ESTIMATES THE amount of savings that you will need to fund your retirement. The important variables you need to input are as follows:

- Your current age
- Age at retirement
- Life expectancy
- Current savings
- Risk appetite: Set by selecting Gear of investing
- Annual savings
- Growth in annual savings
- Inflation rate
- Monthly expenses post-retirement
- Monthly income post-retirement
- Risk appetite post-retirement—set by selecting the right Gear of investing post-retirement

Based on these inputs, the template evaluates whether you have enough savings to last through the expected lifetime. The template is available at https://www.gulaq.com/retirement-planning/.

Children's Education Planning

THIS TEMPLATE USES THE assumptions about the types and costs of education of your children and suggests the savings plan required.

The important variables you need to input are as follows:

- Years to start the course
- Current savings
- Asset allocation
- Inflation
- Cost of education for the type of education you are targeting
- Desired risk level, measured as investment Gear
- Additional annual investment required

Combining these inputs, you can create a plan to save for the goal of your children's education. The template is available at https://www.gulaq.com/children-education-planning/.

Estimating Life Insurance Cover

THIS TEMPLATE ALLOWS YOU to estimate the right amount of life insurance cover that you should purchase.

The important variables you need to input are as follows:

- Your current age
- Your earnings
- Expected growth in your earnings
- Years you plan to work

You can calculate the amount of money you would require if you were to replace a lifetime of earnings with a lumpsum payment now. Of course, the lumpsum payment will be earning returns through proper investments. The template is available at https://www.gulaq.com/estimating-life-insurance-cover/.

Gulaq Gear Selector

THIS TEMPLATE ALLOWS YOU to try out different scenarios with varying levels of investment Gears (risk levels) and whether there is a risk of missing the target amount with a certain asset allocation. The template is available at https://www.gulaq.com/gulaq-gear-selector/.

Glossary

Asset: Something you own that is of value. In the context of investments, stocks, fixed deposits, bonds or real estate would be assets.

Benchmark: The standard which is used to compare the returns of your investment. Typically, for stocks, it would be an index fund covering the universe of stocks that you have invested in.

Bull: A person with an expectation that the market prices will go up from the current levels.

Cash: Money available to spend readily. This includes bank notes, bank account balances and investments like liquid and money market funds.

Dividend: Many companies pay a part of their profits to the shareholders periodically. This is called dividend.

Earnings: Final profit earned by a company after paying all costs, taxes and interest.

Exchange: A marketplace where securities are bought and sold. In India there are several exchanges like NSE, BSE, MCX, MSEI.

Factor: A broad theme of investment like momentum, value, growth.

Gross Return: Return achieved by buying and selling securities, prior to paying any costs, fees and taxes.

Index: A group of securities held in a specific ratio to represent the broad basket of representative securities. Nifty 50 is an index containing the top 50 companies in India and is one of the more popular indices in the Indian stock market.

Large Cap: SEBI defines the top 100 companies as Large Cap.

Liquidity: The ease of converting an investment asset back into cash.

Margin: In futures and options market, an investor needs to pay only a part of the money of the asset. This is called the 'margin'.

Market capitalization: The total value of all the outstanding shares. It is calculated by multiplying the total outstanding shares by the current market price.

Maturity: The time when the duration of investment will be over and the security will be converted back to cash. Typically used in debt instruments to reflect the term of the debt.

Maximum Draw Down (MDD): This means the maximum loss a security can suffer. Measured from the previous high value to the lowest value.

Mid Cap: SEBI defines the companies ranked from 101 to 250 as Mid Cap.

Momentum: Tendency of securities which have increased in price to continue to do so.

Mutual Fund: A portfolio of stocks managed by a professional asset management company in which investors can participate by buying small number of units.

Net Return: The return after paying for costs like fees, transaction costs, government levies, stamp duty, exchange and other charges.

Nifty (also Nifty 50): Index of top 50 stocks on the National Stock Exchange.

Option: A type of market security where the investor has the right to buy or sell an asset but not the obligation.

P/E Ratio: The ratio of the price of a share to its earnings per share.

Portfolio: A basket of securities. Typically selected to create a balance between different market segments and themes.

Return: The profit on the investment, measured as a percentage of the investment.

Risk: Uncertainty in receiving a return. Typically measured as a standard deviation or variance.

Rolling Returns: Investment returns are calculated for a period of, say, 1 month or 1 year. If we want to measure the 12-month return, we can measure the return from January to December or April to March. Every month, we can measure the return of the last 12 months. This is called the rolling return.

Sector Fund: A fund which invests only in companies in a specific sector of the economy. For example, a technology fund will invest only in technology companies.

Security: Any investment product that is bought or sold with an expectation of profit. A share in a company, a government bond, a mutual fund unit are all securities.

Share: A unit of ownership in a business. Also called a stock or equity share.

Small Cap: SEBI defines the companies smaller than the top 250 companies as Small Cap.

Standard Deviation: A measure of how much the returns vary. Mathematical formulas of standard deviation measure the dispersion of returns across the sample.

Technical Analysis: The method of analysing price and volume data to determine the future price of the security.

Total Return: Includes price increase and dividends as well as any other corporate actions.

Tracking Error: A measure of how closely the portfolio tracks the benchmark index. A portfolio that produces returns very different from the benchmark index has a high tracking error. It is measured as the standard deviation of the difference between the portfolio return and the benchmark return.

Value: The earning capacity of a business relative to its price. A business which generates more earnings for the same market cap is considered a better value.

Volatility: The amount of change in prices over time. Usually measured by standard deviation.

Notes

1 I have chosen the name Chanchal which can be for any gender. 'He' is used as a placeholder for 'he', or 'she' or 'they'. This book is addressed to all genders equally.

2 Please refer to the Appendix for an explanation of rolling returns.

3 Data collected from the RBI website.

4 For many who have recently started investing, the answer may be 'b. 5%–7.5%' but that is a historical low.

5 Data sourced from the RBI website: rbi.org.in.

6 This analysis was done using AMFI (Association of Mutual Funds in India) data downloaded from AMFIIndia.com. with performance history from 31 May 2023.

7 'How Gangnam Style Drove an 800% Stock Rise,' *The Wall Street Journal*, 16 October 2013.

8 Eugene F. Fama and Kenneth R. French, 'The Cross-Section of Expected Stock Returns,' *The Journal of Finance*, June 1992.

9 Campbell R. Harvey, Yan Liu, Heqing Zhu, '...and the Cross-Section of Expected Returns,' *The Review of Financial Studies*, Volume 29, Issue 1, January 2016.

10 The amount of savings required is calculated using a statistical estimate of the amount of money needed to meet the goal with 70% certainty under range of market return scenarios. www.gulaq.com/estimating-savings-for-goal/.

About the Author

Sandeep Tyagi lives his life by looking at situations primarily through the lens of analytical thinking. He is a computer engineer from IIT Delhi and an MBA from Columbia University, NY. He built his career helping large companies make decisions using big data. He founded one of the earliest analytics outsourcing companies, Inductis, which he ran for eight years before merging it with EXL Service. He then founded Estee Holdings. Estee is a capital markets firm that makes investment decisions using quantitative methods and executes them using computer systems. Over the years, it has developed leading products in investing and broking using analytics and computer science. More recently, these sophisticated quant algorithms have been packaged into model portfolios for retail investors. Sandeep's passion is to help people invest well. He is happy that his parents, relatives, friends and even his grown children have come to trust his advice.